Where's The Money

Big Dollars to Do Big Business
Like the Big Boys

By Connie Sparks

Win Publishing
Castaic, California

Published by, Win Publishing
27305 W. Live Oak Rd., A-421
Castaic, CA 91384
(661) 208-8229

Editors:
Bonita Early, Editor
Author Scott & Associates

Richard McNally, Copy Editor

Contributions by:
Cal Naulls, First Vice President-Regional Manager
Community Bank

La Kisha Gant, Loan Officer
CDC Small Business Finance

Walter J. Perez, President
Walt Construction

ISBN 13: 978-0-9824077-0-7
ISBN 10: 0-9824077-0-X

To purchase Where's The Money Business Financial Planning System workbook, call 661 208-8229, visit www.wadeinstitute.org or send us an email admin@wadeinstitute.org

Dedication

This book is dedicated to the women in business today, tomorrow and in the future.

Throughout my career as a business consultant and trainer I've encountered some major crossroads with my success. I owe a great deal of gratitude to the women, who embraced me and imparted their knowledge, experiences and success on to me.

And, to my daughters Tonishia, Kenyahta, Connikia and Marvaughn, who are women of today, tomorrow and the future. When no one else believed in me, they did. Their support gave me the strength and motivation to continue my journey and pursuit to happiness.

Table of Contents

Acknowledgements

Many thanks to Cal Naulls, First Vice President- Regional Manager of Community Bank of Santa Clarita Valley, who gave me great insight on the banking industry and how I could best use my skills and knowledge to service the small business community. With his support I was able to meet key people in the banking industry and build mountable business relationships within the Santa Clarita Valley Community.

La Kisha Gant a Loan Officer with the CDC Small Business Finance, who has made herself available to me when I needed an answer to my questions; wanted to close a deal; and with her vast knowledge and experience within the banking industry, showed me how to expand my reach with lenders. Additionally, La Kisha always extended support for my causes and I am truly grateful.

I also want to thank the lenders, my advisory board and business associates for being supportive and seeing my vision to support the small business community.

Authors Preface

When I was a little girl I would stare into space, visualizing what I wanted out of life and how I would someday have my own business and be a successful businesswoman. At the age of sixteen, during the week I would drive into downtown Los Angeles where my cousin worked. For hours I would drive around looking at the tall buildings, fancy stores, and I'd admire the women dressed in business suits. Well, after doing this for about a year, I was so inspired I had made a decision to go after my dream of being a successful businesswoman.

I didn't know how I was going to get there, I just knew I was going to get there. At the age of 22 I launched my first business as a fashion designer. I had a knack for designing. It was tough starting out. I didn't have the capital for most of my materials, but I did have others in the industry who supported my efforts and helped me get what I needed to get started. Finally, I saw my dream come true—a fashion designer, creating trends and dressing women with one-of-a-kind outfits made by me.

It was a dream that lasted about six years. After which time I wasn't able to carry on with my business because I didn't properly plan for the months I didn't make any sales and I didn't project all the stumbles I'd come across in the near future.

Failing with my first venture was a well-learned lesson. I wasn't sure what I did or didn't do wrong, but I knew things didn't quite work out the way I had planned. I did know, it was my destiny to be a successful businesswoman. It was just a matter of learning how to be that woman and lining all my ducks in a row.

I eventually began joining women's network groups (I was always the youngest) where I was able meet established businesswomen and learn the secrets of success. One woman in particular—Diane was her name—owned an accounting firm and was very successful. Diane took me under her wings and began mentoring me. She taught me how to manage my money and invest what little money I did have to work with into my future.

It was because of her that I became fascinated with the idea of investing in my financial independence and learning about financial products the average person wouldn't ever think about or discuss at the dinner table. Unfortunately, Diane moved away and I lost focus of my goals, losing interest in building my wealth.

Well, years later I was back on the bandwagon, putting together my goals, researching, and building relationships with all the right people who had what I wanted and would teach me how to acquire all my desires. It took me a while, but I got it.

Before long I landed a government job in education where I was introduced to 401k retirement funds, tax-sheltered annuities (TSA), and individual retirement accounts (IRA). This is where things really began to look up for me. I educated myself on these products and how I could benefit from them. Shortly thereafter I was introduced to a financial advisor who exposed me to other financial products I hadn't learned about (outside of what Diane had taught me), I hadn't heard of or had even known existed, like government bonds, CDs (certificates of deposit), and treasury notes. He showed me how I could invest in these products on a shoestring budget. So, I opened my first TSA account with a reputable financial institution. Each month I contributed $150 for the first two years and by year three, I had increased my contribution to $300 a month. And you know—the most amazing thing about this investment—I didn't miss the money from my paycheck. It was as if that money never existed, so I was able to manage my take home pay at $300 less than normal.

Before I knew it, in five years I had more than $15,000 sitting in a TSA account, continuing to grow. Although it was established for my retirement, I still had access to use the money for financial hardships or to purchase a home. After losing my job I decided to start another venture. Fortunately, I had this liquid account available to me as I didn't want to take out a loan and rely on institutional funding. Because my business was in the service industry my startup cost was very low. Therefore I only had to withdraw a few thousand to get my home office set up.

I'm just glad that I had financial resources at my disposal. Had I not had this resource, it would have been a challenge starting my business not being able to market my services, purchase supplies and equipment, and continue my education.

Speaking of education, I knew I wanted my children to further their education as well, so I opened an education fund for them. I contributed $75 a month to this account, which grew to more than $5,000 in four years. When my oldest daughter was ready for college, I had no problem covering most of her expenses for the first year (fortunately she was able to get a partial grant).

The moral of this story? It doesn't' take much to figure out how to become financially solvent. Investing a few dollars a month in your future could make all the difference in your life. Once you begin to understand the vitality of planning and financial independence you will start to see a change in how you conduct business and save money.

What's greater than being a self-made success? Is it easy? No. Does it require work on your part? Yes. Think about the rewards—power and control—that come with financial independence. Know that "everything is possible and nothing is impossible."

According to Robert Castiglione, author of *The Key to Financial Success*, the four rules for personal financial success are:

1. Money is a commodity; it is not simply a number.

2. Money is precious and finite; it must be treated as a precious commodity and protected against all eroding factors.

3. Money must be used efficiently and effectively; it must not be left to just accumulate over time, nor should it be set aside for just one purpose.

4. Money must be respected and must be put to work for the good of society as well as for your own financial future.

Making money should be a priority. Let your money work for you. As you read through the chapters of my book you will discover many financial products, which can help you achieve financial freedom. This would require no more than a small commitment to make it happen. I'm sure one day you would like your business to work for you instead of you working for it.

Today, more and more entrepreneurs are self-funding their business, using cash from savings, taking out home-equity loans or HELOC's, and draining credit cards to fulfill their life-long dream of owning a business. I admire those who are relentless in their efforts to finance their business at all costs after being turned down for a loan.

There are so many alternatives to financing your business, save for retirement, and fund your children's education. If you want to win the battle between success and failure, consider making a change in the way you think about money, how you spend it, how you save it, and where you put it. The effects of having a personal financial model and reserves can be a rewarding experience for you, your family and your business.

If you are truly serious about acquiring financial independence, this is the time to start investing in your future and do what the Big Boys have been doing for many years.

1. They built a sound financial foundation with financial products one investment at a time using diversified planning tools.

2. They saved and spent their money wisely.

3. They stayed abreast on all the latest news and changes in the economy.

4. They took advantage of financial resources available to them.

5. They had a plan.

6. They created the ideal financial portfolio.

Introduction

♦♦♦♦♦♦♦♦♦♦♦♦♦♦♦♦♦♦♦♦♦♦♦♦♦♦♦♦♦♦♦

You should read this book if you are open minded and have aspirations and goals to be financially solvent in your personal and business affairs.

You should read this book if you want to learn how to weather the storm of an economic downturn, want to retire and live the lifestyle you desire, and save for your child's education.

You should read this book if you want to find more ways to increase your inflow of cash.

If any of any of the above apply to you—this book is the perfect book to get started and on your way to financial independence.

The format of this book is unlike the typical how-to book**.** ***Where's the Money*** talks about the 5 Ws and the H:

- Who
- What
- Where
- Why
- When and
- How

The information is straight to the point. You won't find lengthy lectures or wordy examples. I don't want to lose you and I don't want to confuse you. I do want to educate you; I want you to be able to apply the information as it suits your needs, setting the stage for a successful outcome.

After reading *Where's the Money*—you will have a keen understanding of:

- How to improve your cash flow.
- How to turn your business into a bankable business.
- Financial products on the market.
- How to strategically search for and secure loans.
- All the loan products available.
- How the big boys make their money.
- What lenders look for in a business and proposal.
- How to read financial projections and
- How to get the money.

Where's the Money?

Oftentimes I get the question, "Connie, where is all the money?" I say, the money is in the lining pocket linings of investors, institutions, and government and corporations. The question is not where's the money—it's how do I get the money. I could blab off dozens of resources to find the money, then what? Now you know where to find the money—where do you go from there?

Securing or generating an infusion of cash comes in two folds:

1. You need to know where to get the money.
2. How to get it.

One makes no sense without the other.

We all have dreams and goals; conversely to realize them you must act on them. It can be tough reaching for the stars if you don't have the right ladder with adequate steps to help you reach them.

No one said life would be easy, however as history has shown us—you can achieve, be, and have anything you want as long as you are willing to do what it takes to get it. This may require you being money smart—setting financial goals, working on a budget, and letting your money work for you. Put your money some place where it can earn money without you having to do anything other than letting it sit in a money recycling system.

Money recycling systems are savings accounts, investment accounts, retirement accounts, etc., which can give you an edge on life and offer financial independence to help you achieve your financial goals. Unfortunately, with all the services, training, and programs available to people, there's still one area educators, service organizations, and the government fail to invest more time and resource in—FINANCIAL LITERACY.

When I say FINANCIAL LITERACY, I'm not talking about accounting or banking. I'm talking about what makes the world go round—learning how to mange your money, how to spend it wisely, and understanding the power of having money. We as a society should understand the existence of our economy, which depends on the circulation of money, money which flows in so that it can flow out. And the existence of our livelihood, which depends on how well we plan, save, and use our money. If you're not taught or given the tools, how can you save, earn and make money for a better living.

Without financial literacy and understanding, our lives would be a constant shift to nowhere.

How to Use a Financial Portfolio

What is a Financial Portfolio? It's a smart financial planning model, a strategy designed to help you acquire security, growth, and wealth using a variety of financial products. It can also be used as secured collateral to borrow capital from a bank for operations, to purchase commercial property, to expand your business or for real estate investments. A financial portfolio integrates the use of multiple asset-based products such as securities, bonds, certificates of deposit, and mutual and money market funds, which generate a flow of cash through them. Some portfolios perform with greater risk than others, which can vary according to your comfort level.

So, first things first: You must use due diligence and find out what financial products best suit your financial goals. This is not a one-size-fits-all deal. Your needs may differ from someone else's. You should have clarity and understand all of your options when building your portfolio.

Where's The Money is not a how-to-get-rich-quick or a money-making investment book. It is a financial literacy resource designed for the common person who has an open mind and is interested in being informed and educated about financial products, financing opportunities, and strategies to improve any financial short falls for growth and prosperity.

Have you ever wondered how the wealthy got wealthy? They knew how to play the game, where to find the money, and they learned how to use simple strategies—buying bank products, purchasing bonds and treasuries, and taking their profits and investing in other opportunities such as the secondary market. Eventually their small investments grew into larger investments, which made an influx of securities available to own, buy, and build corporate America.

You don't have to spend hundreds or even thousands to gain wealth. It's all in how you allocate your assets, diversify, and ladder products for maximum growth.

I will show you how you can build your business using creative strategies to secure capital, coupling information from various sections in my book. Strategies will vary and should be addressed accordingly. Moreover, you will learn about loan products other than your traditional SBA loans; what lenders look for in a worthy borrower; the various types of lenders; how to create a bankable proposal lenders will look at; and how to determine if you're bankable by using the same evaluation forms lenders use.

There are also strategies for those who are credit challenged and may not qualify for conventional funding.

Accessing capital or transforming yourself into a self- made success should not be a job. I want you, the common person living from paycheck to paycheck and robbing Peter to pay Paul, to live abundantly and take advantage of the same opportunities as your counterparts.

This is a one of a kind book, filled with informative scenarios you can use for personal use or business. By applying the methods and strategies accordingly, you will soon find yourself on the road to financial recovery.

Each chapter will provide you with descriptive information about each topic, do's and don'ts, how best to use the instrument, and its advantages and disadvantages.

Although this book is intended to educate you and illustrate the use of the mentioned products, it should not be misconstrued as financial advisement. It is merely a road map to achieving your financial goals and financial success.

A Self-Made Success Story

W*here's the Money* is about transforming you into a self-made success. Over the past eight years I've searched for the 21st Century self-made successor with an intriguing story to share. Then I met him. It was during the course of researching material for this book. When I first heard his story, I was blown away and wanted to share his success story with other business owners and entrepreneurs.

I could not have finished this book without this interview. I wanted to show you it is possible, no matter what stage in life or business you are in right now, that success is always standing by.

I want to share with you his interview and how he transformed himself into a self-made success. His name is Walter J. Perez, president of Walt Construction and here is his story.

CS: How did Walter J. Perez become a self-made success?
WJP: For starters it goes back to the basics of devising a plan with a viable product and some idea of how to execute the plan and move forward. I started my first business at the age of thirteen-years old, living in Peru, South America. One-day while at the movies there was a disco party scene with these psychedelic lights and I was intrigued by them. I went home, couldn't sleep from thinking about these lights and said "I have to make those lights because they are fun", so when I have a party I could have these lights.

So, I went to work and built a box with lights, which took about a month and then built another set of lights with different colors, so now I had two sets of multi-color lights. My friend had a party and I brought the lights, which made the party a success. I then began thinking-what if I could have one at every party in town? (Everyone uses regular on and off switch lights) this could be a major success if I were to make more lights and rent them.

Around the age of 14, I had about eight or nine sets of lights and started renting them out on Friday and Saturday nights. At the age of 14 I was making a lot more money than the average adult person made. Unfortunately, I was a kid and blew all my money.

What I took from this, was the concept of business-there's something that people need-that's a product and that was the idea based on the movie I saw. Therefore, I decided to make a plan to implement the boxes and began executing that idea and turned it into a business.

I started renting to parties and targeting 15-year-old girls who would soon have sweet 16 parties and this was the beginning of my business. This is how you do business and turn a product and a service into income. By the age of 16 my parents wanted to move to the United States, and I turned the business over to a relative.

This was my first experience in business, I made a lot of money and thought that was a unique and one-time thing. As I got older I realized that was the same principal in business-to come up with an idea of a product or service, create a plan, implement it and execute it.

CS: Did you have a traditional business plan or just a plan?
WJP: Not a traditional plan, in fact my plan wasn't written, it was in my head and I knew what I wanted to do. Although, the principal of doing business and having a plan existed, I was able to be successful because I knew what demographics I wanted to target, I knew how I was going to market my product. I targeted young girls in the seventh and eight grade, turning sweet 16. This was the perfect time to target them. I went to schools, passed out fliers and showed pictures of other parties-marketing my product and services. I knew the girls would encourage their parents to hire me, because no one else had these lights in town.

CS: So you created a unique product no one else had?
WJP: A very unique product and knew how to market it to a very specific demographic. So, I have followed that same principal today.

CS: After coming to the United States, what did you do?
WJP: Attended college with a major in photography-didn't finish- I realized it wasn't for me. I'm a hands-on person and wanted to do something which was constructive and I needed to produce something. I took on a job in the lighting industry making lights for parties. I also liked electrical, so I got a part-time job as an electrician, which turned into full-time and that turned into a career for me. So, school became secondary to me. I did however, take classes I wanted and needed such as law classes, engineering, management, and technical classes. I basically learned what I needed and wanted to learn to complement what I do.

By the age of 22, I said this was my time, I'm getting old and if I don't start doing something now, then when. So, I founded an industrial company, California Industrial Electrical Corporation. I started the company with one employee and myself. By year four I had 100 employees, ever since the company has been very strong and doing a lot of business even in this downward economy.

CS: How did you finance your first company- California Industrial Electrical?
WJP: I started with $20,000 from savings, bought a truck, a telephone system and a couple desks, and I worked out of my garage. Every dollar the company made, 100% was reinvested back into the company. I took very little money for myself, could have bought a big house within the first year in business and new cars, but I said no, I'm not going to do that, I'm going to stay in my little house. I did move out of the garage into my first office space with a shop. I was very thrifty with my personal and business expenses. I drove the same pickup truck I had for five years, for a long-time.

Additionally I started doing something that most people don't do-I paid myself first. Usually when people get a payment from a contract the first thing they do is pay their bills, after all the bills are paid whatever is left is theirs. I look at things a little different. Before any payments go out-I Walter J. Perez have to get paid. I worked a month, two months for this project and there is a value for my work.

So what I do is take a percentage of the payment, depending on the profits of the project and that is a payment I make to myself, because I am worth something. I assess the value of my efforts and pay it. It could be made to a personal savings account or the company's savings account at 6%-8%, which ever way, me or the company gets paid first, and what ever is left is distributed to other accounts (of course I have to make sure there's enough money to cover costs).

There is a big balance of 92%-94% left so that everyone else gets paid. So, following that principle, if you were to take a percentage off the top, you will start getting used to it. No matter how much it is. And the balance goes into other designated accounts, you will get use to it as it becomes a natural order to ensure you get paid for your efforts. After a while you won't even realize you're actually earning a percentage.

The bottom-line is the company needs to be cash strong, we all need money, we need to self finance ourselves through our own profits. I put this money aside and I do make this money work for me through mutual funds, buying commercial property, and historically buy cars and trucks we need with cash. We don't get financing from the banks we have our own little car account that we put money into every month. When the company say's we need a new pick up truck, we pay cash.

The only time we finance is when the manufacturer provides a zero to three percent financing, we'll take full advantage of that. We will not consider a conventional loan at five to eight percent. We save our money. Instead of the money going to some finance guy in New York, collecting interest, we collect our own interest in essence. We self finance ourselves.

CS: Do you have an itemized budget for accounts for specific uses?
WJP: We do more than that. We have accounts for equipment, trucks, and tools. We know that in one year's time tools will need to be replaced or the lifetime for a Backhoe is approximately ten years and will need to be replaced at that time. Well, having these reserved accounts allow the company to be prepared when a piece of equipment needs to be replaced. Instead of buying a Backhoe on credit paying thousands a month, I'd rather save the interest cost. In ten years that money will have grown, because I invested it in any which way I can, therefore we make money on our own money rather than pay it out.

CS: Are all of your accounts set up in a mutual fund allowing your money to work for you?
WJP: Lately, instead of putting money into mutual funds, we are investing in real estate. Borrowing moneys for Real Estate purchases is necessary and the properties must create their own income.

CS: You mentioned you have another company. When did you form it and how did it come about?
WJP: About four years ago I started looking into opening new companies, so I decided instead of opening a new company why don't I just buy a company that's been in business for a longtime. At that point we bought an older company that had been in business since 1975, and renamed it Walt Construction Corporation.

It was a good company with mostly bad accounts, which we Cleaned up and kept the good accounts. We needed their long-term establishment, which was in good standing since 1975 and their experience in the building industry.

CS: Do you have ownership in any other company's?
WJP: There is one more, its called Axim Systems Corporation. We did the same thing with this company as Walt Construction. It had been in business for 25 years, we bought them out two years ago.

CS: How do you balance the three companies?
WJP: Work long hours, hiring the right people, hiring the right crew, management, and having an accounting system that can take on the extra work.

CS: How many employees do you currently have compared to when you first started your business?
WP: A lot less than when I started.

CS: Why is that?
WJP: We're working smarter. We are able to take advantage of all our resources. We sub out a lot of the work to other companies and use their resources and their payroll, which means they have to carry their own cost. So, we've been really successful at tapping into other company's resources and successes. That's why we have less employees, less trucks, and less equipment.

CS: When did you decided to reduce staff and take advantage of your resources to make this change work for you?
WJP: In 1990 my entire business was based on doing work for Aerospace and we grew quite a bit and I realized we were in financial trouble. When I was younger even though I reinvested the money, I didn't have a lot of savings. I figured the money was going to keep coming and we're a rich company and don't have to worry about saving anything. It was a part of our learning experience.

In 1991 I realized not many companies were excelling and growing at that time. Everybody was in trouble without work. There may have been three or four companies growing at that time and I couldn't understand how in a bad economy companies could grow while everyone is without work. Well, today we are one of those companies. When the economy is so bad and there's no work our company keeps growing. By modeling what those other companies were doing and understand why, in two years I figured out and began implementing their strategy.

It all came down to money. Those companies saved their money, put money on the side, put money in their own savings account and investments, and not heavily financed. They had a lot of cash and when the bottom fell they were very strong and were able to go to their clients and new clients and say "we are very strong, here's our proof-look at our financials, if you give us the job we can guarantee we'll finish the work", while the competition is weak and in financial troubles. Prospects couldn't rely on companies that were not financially strong, because there were no guarantees the work would be completed.

CS: Where do you see all three companies in the next five years?
WJP: I foresee a lot of growth. I have studied all my competition, what makes them successful and not successful. I constantly observe them at what they do and don't do. I don't want to reinvent the wheel I. All I'm doing is looking at what works and following through. Very basic stuff there's no science to this. I model the platforms larger company's are using and implement them in my own companies.

It comes down to some very basic principals-saving your earnings-a small percentage and building up your cash.

Are You Prepared for the Challenge?

CHAPTER 1

BUILDING A FINANCIAL PORTFOLIO

More than 90 percent of the business community falls short when it comes to financial planning. Many small businesses rely on cash infusion from the government or conventional lending institutions, seeking financial assistance in the form of a loan. Don't get me wrong, if you can get it, get it.

Nevertheless, there are more unqualified business owners than qualified who are less likely able to receive funding for their business.

Approximately 80 percent of the business community does not qualify for SBA or conventional funding because of poor credit, no assets, or no injection (down payment). So, what's a business to do to be successful and financially solvent? I say invest in the future and independence. Build a diverse financial portfolio you can use as leverage to access additional capital when needed.

The goal is to create a long-term financial growth strategy and:

- have assets to capitalize on
- create financial independence and security
- use it to secure capital through conventional or unconventional means
- create viability in the business and
- THINK BIG

Wouldn't it be great to walk into a bank or approach an investor and say I need $300,000? A financial portfolio is one of many ways to achieve this. If you have less than perfect credit, no injection, or no real collateral, owning other assets such as securities can open many doors.

Note: The following information is for informational purposes only. Please seek advice from a professional financial advisor before making investment decisions.

The following products I call "Forgotten: the best kept secrets" Because most advisors, CPAs, and brokers don't bother to discuss these options with the common person who cannot open accounts in excess of $10,000 or more. I think it's a farce that advisors don't consider discussing all financial growth opportunities with a client, no matter his or her current situation. Today may not be the opportune time, however tomorrow just may be. If small business owners were informed of these options, it would make planning a lot easier.

These products have been in existence since the mid 1800s, yet today we are just learning of them and how to use them. I believe if more efforts went into teaching financial literacy the economy and business community would be much stronger forces, capable of weathering any storm.

Here's to educating you and keeping you informed. You will learn the fundamentals of owning financial products the big boys use to plan short-term and long-term.

Mutual Funds

What Is A Mutual Fund?

A mutual fund is just a convenient package or basket of a lot of investments—mainly stocks and bonds, which could be complicated for the typical investor to manage otherwise. Mutual funds are the way the masses invest in the stock market. They are a cheap, easy and efficient way for people without a lot of money or financial experience to take advantage of stocks and bonds.

Mutual funds employ professional managers to oversee the operations. ING Direct (Sharebuilder.com) is a great resource to start investing. To open an account cost's as little as $50. Many mutual funds are highly diversified in their investments, meaning they own shares in a number of different industries and in small, medium and large companies. In the event one or more of the stocks are struggling they won't dramatically affect the whole fund.

Mutual Fund companies with fund managers are very convenient. They do most of the record keeping for you and provide you with the forms needed to file your taxes. In addition, many offer services such as check writing against a money market fund and other bells and whistles.

There are three types of mutual funds, which include stocks, bonds, and money market. Many investors mix the three for a more diversified portfolio, which can balance investment growth.

Let's begin with Stock Funds

Stock funds, also called equity funds, are the most volatile of the three (will discuss later), with their value sometimes rising and falling sharply over a short period. But historically stocks have performed better over the long term than other types of investments. Stocks are traded with the presumption that a company will generate higher revenues and higher profits, which would increase shareholder value.

One of the beauties of owning stock in a company—you are not only a consumer of the product you now own a piece of the company which produces the product. This gives you voting rights (depending if your shares are preferred or common) and makes you money as the company makes money.

Generally stocks fluctuate because of investors' assessment of economic conditions and their likely impact on corporate earnings. A responsible investor will factor in other risks to earnings such as exposure to fines or lawsuits from polluting the environment or discriminating against particular employees. Not all stock funds are the same.

Some common funds include:

- Growth funds, which offer the potential for large capital appreciation but may not pay a regular dividend.

- Income funds that invest in stocks that pay regular dividends.

- Index funds, which try to mirror the performance of a particular market index, such as the S&P 500 Composite Stock Price Index.

- Sector funds usually specialize in a particular industry segment, such as finance, health care or technology

Stock accounts can be opened through an investment broker or you can simply manage these funds yourself online through services such as ING Direct, Etrade or Scott Trade (that is if you have the time and skills). The cost to start up an account will vary. They can range from $50 to $1,000, depending on your investment style.

Bond Funds

There are many types of bonds. However here we will discuss Bond Funds. To ensure investing in the right bond (s), be sure to research and learn their advantages and disadvantages. Conversely, evaluate your needs both short term and long term.

Why Buy Bonds?

Bond funds are often included in a portfolio to boost an investor's total return by providing steady income when stock funds lose value. Bond funds are known as fixed income You can invest in corporate and government debt with the purpose of providing income through dividend payments.

Like stock funds, which can be organized by sector, bond funds too can be categorized. They can range in risk from low to risky. U.S.-backed Treasury bonds are considered low risk and junk bonds, are considered high risk and have a lower credit rating than investment-grade corporate bonds.

Just like any investment, whether stocks, real estate, or funds, bonds too have risk:

- The possibility the issuer may fail to pay back their debt;

- The possibility interest rates will rise, which causes the value of the bonds to decline;

- The possibility a bond will be paid off early. When that happens within bond funds there is the chance the manager may not be able to reinvest the proceeds in something else that pays as high a return.

Money Market Funds
Money market funds have relatively low risks, compared to other mutual funds and most other investments. By law they are limited to investing only in specific high-quality, short-term investments issued by the U.S. government, U.S. corporations, and state and local governments.

Money market funds try to keep their "net asset value" (NAV) — which represents the value of one share in a fund — at a constant $1 per share. But the NAV may fall below $1 if the fund's investments perform poorly.

Money market accounts can be opened with as little as $100. Check with bankrate.com for banks and institutions offering the best return rates.

Do Your Due Diligence
The most important thing you should do as a money market fund investor is to visit one of the main mutual fund rating sites such as S&P or Fitch's. If you're looking for a safer place to invest cash assets, you should always look for top-rated money market funds.

Other forms of investments to consider are T-Bills and Savings Bonds. You don't here much of these investments throughout in general. That's because the common businessperson or consumer will watch the news to hear about the latest hit story in the community (which is important) and fail to watch the business news (MSNBC, CNN) keeping abreast on issues relating to the economy, their industry, and changes, which can impact their business.

If you can, dedicate at least one to two hours every morning watching the business news and reading the newspaper. Years ago, I was one of those who didn't see the significance in reading the newspaper every single day. Until my boyfriend purchased a subscription to the LA Times, and sat me down every morning with him to read the paper. And, wouldn't you know it-not only did I learn about what was going on in the world-I discovered opportunities.

For example, a new hotel had recently opened in a near by city and was looking for businesses to patronize it's conference and banquet rooms at a discount rate. At that time I just launched a new program and was looking for company's I could partner with and was interested in exposure and free marketing. So, I called the Sales Manager, and the rest is history. Now I host my clinics at a reputable chain hotel, utilizing a small space (at no charge) and Wa-la! Both the hotel and I are benefiting from this partnership.

I hope that I was able to get my point across, about educating yourself and creating opportunities when you least expect to.

Back to bonds. Bills and bonds are typically discussed at luncheons, gala's, or dinners whereas political figures, corporate executives, financial advisors, and high net-worth investors congregate.

Turn this into a regular table conversation with your spouse, children and friends. Children too should also learn how to invest into their future and start saving where it counts. It's time for change, knowledge is power, and this is how we as a whole can contribute to the wealth of our communities.

Treasury Bills

Treasury bills, or T-bills, are sold in terms ranging from a few days to 52 weeks. Bills are typically sold at a discount from the par amount (also called face value). For instance, you might pay $990 for a $1,000 bill. When the bill matures, you would be paid $1,000. The difference between the purchase price and face value is interest. It is possible for a bill auction to result in a price equal to par, which means that Treasury will issue and redeem the securities at par value.

Bills can be purchased at minimum $100

Treasury Notes

Treasury notes, sometimes called T-Notes, earn a fixed rate of interest every six months, annually until maturity. Notes are issued in terms of 2, 3, 5, and 10 years. To buy a Treasury note through the U.S. Treasury, you place a competitive or noncompetitive bid for the note: Minimum Purchase $100. You also can purchase notes through a bank, broker or govex. Govex is an online agency registered with the government. Investors can sell or buy U.S. Small Business Administration's 7a guaranteed loans. You can hold a note until it matures or sell it before maturity back to the original holder.

Treasury Bonds

Treasury bonds pay a fixed rate of interest every six months until they mature. They are issued in a term of 30 years. When a bond matures, the owner is paid the face value of the bond. Bonds can be held until maturity or sold on the market before maturity.

Minimum Term of Ownership: None
Interest Earning Period: To maturity

Interest income is exempt from state and local income taxes. Interest income is subject to federal income tax.

Another consideration, if you really want to get serious about investing: try your hand at Treasury Inflation-Protected Securities, one of many debt investment products you can choose from to gain dollar for dollar on your investment.

Treasury Inflation-Protected Securities (TIPS)
The most popular class of inflation-hedge bonds that protect investors from inflation risk are the extremely safe fixed-income investments from the U.S. Treasury Department known as TIPS, or Treasury Inflation-Protected Securities.

When you buy a TIPS, you don't have to worry that the face value of the security will decline in an inflationary economy. The principal in a TIPS is adjusted semiannually to reflect rises in the Consumer Price Index.

More importantly, the reverse is **not** true. If the economy were to become deflationary, the principal of the TIPS is not reduced. The government guarantees that at least the face value of a TIPS will be paid upon maturity.

Treasury Inflation-Protected Securities, or TIPS, provide protection against inflation. The principal of a TIPS increases with inflation and decreases with deflation, as measured by the Consumer Price Index. When a TIPS matures, you are paid the adjusted principal or the original principal, whichever is greater.

TIPS pay interest twice a year, at a fixed rate. The rate is applied to the adjusted principal; so, like the principal, interest payments rise with inflation and fall with deflation.

Use TIPS to:

- Diversify your investment portfolio
- Supplement retirement income

Minimum Term of Ownership: None
Interest Earning Period: To maturity

Interest income and growth in principal are exempt from state and local income taxes but are subject to federal income tax.

TIPS are sold directly by the Treasury Department in the month in which they are issued. Those sales are free of fees and commissions. Every penny you spend on a TIPS will be invested in the TIPS. To buy directly from the federal government, you'll need to sign up for the Treasurydirect.gov program at www.treasurydirect.gov.com.

Many experts advise individual investors to purchase TIPS through mutual funds rather than buying individual securities because you'll benefit from the wide array of TIPS held in the fund. Buying individual TIPS can be very expensive because the minimum purchase price is $1,000.

There's an important difference to remember when buying individual TIPS vs. buying a TIPS bond fund. You're always certain of getting your full principal if you hold an individual bond until maturity. If you Sell before maturity you'll get the current price and risk-losing your principal.

Another unspoken of product: Revenue Anticipation Notes (RANs), one of the few notes exempt from taxation. It matures in 12 months at full value.

I Savings Bonds

I Bonds are low-risk, liquid savings products. While you own them they earn interest and protect you from inflation. You may purchase I Bonds via Treasurydirect.gov, at most local financial institutions or through payroll deduction. Minimum purchase $25 at face value.

The bond world offers a number of hedges against inflation. The cost and risks vary. IBonds are a form of U.S. Savings Bond. They're backed by the full faith and credit of the U.S. Government and are seen as extremely safe investments.

Use I Bonds to:

- Finance education
- Supplement retirement income
- Give as a gift

Rates and Terms

- I Bonds have an annual interest rate that reflects the combined effects of a fixed rate and a semiannual inflation rate. They are an accrual-type security. Interest is added to the bond monthly and is paid when you cash the bond.
- I Bonds are sold at face value; i.e., you pay $50 for a $50 bond.

Redemption Information

- Minimum term of ownership: 1 year
- Interest-earning period: 30 years
- Early redemption penalties:
  - ❖ Before 5 years, forfeit 3 most recent months' interest
  - ❖ After 5 years, no penalty

Tax Considerations

- Interest earnings are exempt from state and local income taxes, but are subject to state and local estate, inheritance, gift, and other excise taxes.
- Interest earnings are subject to federal income tax.
- Interest earnings may be excluded from federal income tax when used to finance education.

"BONDS"?

Question: What is a Bond?

Answer: A Bond is simply an 'IOU' in which an investor agrees to loan money to a company or government at a predetermined interest rate.

If a business wants to expand, one of its options is to borrow money from individual investors. The company issues bonds at various interest rates and sells them to the public. Investors purchase them with the understanding that the company will pay back their original principal plus any interest that is due by a set date (this is called the "maturity).

The interest a bondholder earns depends on the strength of the corporation. For example, a blue chip is more stable and has a lower risk of defaulting on its debt. When companies such as Microsoft, IBM, etc., issue bonds, they may only pay seven percent interest, while a much less stable start-up pays ten percent. A general rule of thumb when investing in bonds is "the higher the interest rate, the riskier the bond."

Who can issue bonds? Governments, municipalities, a variety of institutions, and corporations. "Commercial Paper" is simply referring to bonds issued by companies. There are many types of bonds, each having different features and characteristics. A few of the most notable are zero coupon and convertible.

Municipal Bonds (Muni Bonds)

Non-profit organizations are almost always better off investing in corporate bonds due to their tax-free status. Investors in high-income brackets are almost always better off investing in tax-free municipal bonds.

Municipal bonds, or "munis" for short, are IOUs issued by city, county, and state governments in order to raise money for community projects such as a highway, a new school, or a hospital. Their primary attraction is that the interest paid to the owner of a municipal bond is exempt from federal taxes. In most cases, interest is exempt from state taxes as well if the investor resides within the same state in which the municipal bonds were issued.

EE/E Savings Bonds

Series EE savings bonds are safe, low-risk savings products that pay interest based on current market rates for up to 30 years for bonds purchased May 1997 through April 30, 2005. You may purchase EE Bonds via Treasurydirect.gov or at almost any financial institution or through your employer's payroll deduction plan, if available.

Use EE Bonds to:

- Finance education
- Supplement retirement income
- Give as a gift

How It Works:

You pay $25 for a $50 EE Bond when purchasing paper bond certificates

You pay $25 for a $25 EE bond when purchased electronically via Treasury Direct

Maximum Purchase (per calendar year):
$5,000 in Treasury Direct and $5,000 in paper bonds (purchase price)

Paper Bonds Denominations: $50, $74, $100, $200, $500, $1,000, $5,000, and $10,000

Issue Method: Electronic bonds via Treasury Direct: purchase to the penny for $25 or more paper bond certificates or Electronic issue in Treasury Direct accounts

Rates & Terms

- They are an accrual-type security, which means interest is added to the bond monthly and paid when you cash in the bond.
- Paper bonds are sold at half the face value; i.e., you pay $25 for a $50 bond.
- Electronic bonds purchased via Treasury Direct are sold at face value.

Redemption Information

- Minimum term of ownership: 1 year
- Interest-earning period: 30 years
- Early redemption penalties:
    - ❖ Before 5 years, forfeit 3 most recent months' interest
    - ❖ After 5 years, no penalty

Tax Considerations

- Interest earnings are exempt from state and local income taxes, but are subject to federal, state, and local estate, inheritance, gift, and other excise taxes.
- Interest earnings are subject to federal income tax.
- Interest earnings may be excluded from federal income tax when bonds are used to finance education (see education tax exclusions). Restrictions apply.

Okay, now that you've learned about a few products and how they work let's talk about how to use them and make them work for you.

Asset Allocation

Asset allocation means dividing your investments into several different categories to protect your portfolio and create a balance when the market swings in one direction. Asset allocation is the single most important factor in being a successful investor.

How much you invest in each chosen category is the process of asset allocation. For the most part you want to mix your portfolio with stocks, bonds, and cash.

For example, you may decide your particular financial situation calls for a mix of 70 percent stocks, 20 percent bonds, and 10 percent cash. You might further break it down this way:

Stocks 70%	**Bonds 20%**	**Cash 10%**
Income 20%	Long-Term 15%	Short-Term Bond Fund 10%
Growth 30%	Mid-Term 5%	
Foreign 10%		
Small-Cap 10%		
Total: 70%	**Total: 20%**	**Total: 10%**

These are hypothetical numbers. You should always base your allocation and investments on the following:

- Risk tolerance
- Income
- Savings
- Retirement goal
- Available cash flow
- Economy

Things To Remember:

- Asset allocation is the process of splitting your investments among stocks, bonds, and cash.
- A properly balanced portfolio can help protect you from severe market fluctuations.
- Risk tolerance plays a big role in portfolio selection.
- Splitting your assets among different investment categories helps you weather the ups and downs that are part of the investing cycle.
- Look at your portfolio at least once a quarter for proper balance—more frequently in turbulent markets.

Certificates of Deposit (CD)

One of the most common fixed-income investments is a Certificate of Deposit (CD). A CD is a long-term investment that has a higher yield.

A CD is an excellent way to save money and earn a higher interest rate than you would with most money market investments. The drawback is that you're tying up your funds for a period of time and if you cash out early you'll lose interest and possibly principal.

How It Works
You invest a fixed amount of money for a period of time called the term, and you're guaranteed your principal plus a fixed amount of interest in return. The term can be 3-months to 5-years. When the term expires you can cash out the principal and interest, or roll over the CD for another term. You can opt to withdraw the interest payments as they are received.

Generally, you should not buy a CD with a term of more than five years. The interest rate could change dramatically during that time and you could get stuck with a long-term, low-rate CD.

CDs are deposit accounts and are insured by the Federal Deposit Insurance Corporation, up to $100,000 ($250,000 on retirement accounts). On October 3, 2008, FDIC deposit insurance temporarily increased from $100,000 to $250,000 per depositor through December 31, 2009.

Types of CDs
There are traditional and nontraditional CDs offered at selected financial institutions. Traditional CDs are most common. You can find some nontraditional CDs with high-yield risk and flexibility that may be suitable for your financial needs.

The traditional certificate of deposit remains the most popular type of CD, but a growing number of financial institutions are offering a variety of nontraditional CDs that have an element of flexibility. If you're willing to sacrifice some yield, you can find CD options that might better suit your financial needs.

Traditional
Deposit a fixed amount of money for a specific term and receive a predetermined interest rate. You have the option of cashing out at the end of the term or rolling over the CD for another term. Most institutions allow you to add additional funds during the term or when rolling over. Penalties for early withdrawal can be quite stiff and will cause you to lose interest and, possibly, principal. Federal regulations stipulate only the minimum early withdrawal penalty. There is no law preventing an institution from enacting tougher penalties, but they must be disclosed when the account is opened.

Bump-up
These allow you to take advantage of a rising rate environment. Suppose you buy a two-year CD at a given rate and six months into the term the bank is offering an additional quarter-point on two-year CDs. A bump-up CD gives you the option of telling the bank you want to get the higher rate for the remainder of the term. Institutions that offer this option usually allow one bump-up per term.

The drawback is you may get a lower initial rate than on a traditional two-year CD. The longer it takes interest rates to rise, the higher they'll have to go to make up for the earlier, lower-rate portion of the term. So, be sure you have realistic expectations about the interest rate environment before buying a bump-up CD.

Liquid
These offer consumers the opportunity to withdraw money from the CD without incurring a penalty, however you may have to maintain a minimum balance in the account to get that privilege. The interest rate on a liquid CD should be higher than the bank's money market rate, but would usually be lower than a traditional CD of the same term and minimum.

A key consideration when purchasing a liquid CD is how soon after opening the account you'll be able to make a withdrawal. Federal law requires that the money stay in the account for seven days before it can be withdrawn without penalty, but banks can set the first penalty-free withdrawal for any period beyond that.

Another consideration is the number of withdrawals allowed. You'll have to weigh the convenience of liquidity against whatever return you're sacrificing when compared to similar term CDs without the liquidity feature.

Zero-coupon
Most investors have heard of zero-coupon bonds, but did you know there are also zero-coupon CDs? Just as with a bond, you buy the CD at a deep discount to par value (the amount you'll get when the CD matures). The word "coupon" refers to an interest payment. Zero-coupon means no interest payments.

For example, if you buy a 5-year, $100,000 CD with a 7 percent interest rate for $50,000, you wouldn't receive any interest payments during the 5-year term. Instead, that money is being invested. The problem is you will have appreciation income each year. No money is being put in your pocket but you have to pay Uncle Sam because you owe tax on the interest. You would owe taxes the first year on $3,500 you haven't actually received. Each year you'll have a higher base than the year before—and a bigger tax bill. Make sure you have the funds to cover the taxes.

Callable
The bank that issues the CD can "call" it away from you after the call-protection expires, but before the CD matures. For instance, if you buy a five-year CD with a six-month call protection period, it would be callable after the first six months.

What's happening here is the bank is shifting interest rate risk onto your shoulders. If they issue the CD at 5 percent and six months later rates drop and the bank is now paying 4 percent on five-year CDs, the bank can call, or take back, your CD and reissue it at 4 percent. Of course, you'll receive your full principal and interest earned to date. They may pay a quarter or half-percent more on a callable CD than they would on a CD without the call feature.

Brokerage

A brokerage CD is simply a CD sold through a brokerage. Some banks use brokers as sales representatives to find investors willing to purchase CDs from their banks. Brokered CDs often pay higher rates than CDs from your local bank because banks using brokered CDs compete in a national marketplace. These CDs are more liquid than bank CDs because they can be traded like bonds on the secondary market, but there is no guarantee you won't take a loss. The only way to guarantee getting your full principal and interest is to hold the CD until it matures. Brokered CDs often have call options and they're backed by the FDIC.

Venturing into the investment game you must be savvy in your strategy and have fixed income investments to sustain the ups and downs of the market. Or, you can opt for solid Certificates of Deposit.

Here is a strategy I discovered from a financial advisor. This is one of the most realistic strategies I've heard of during my research. Remember, having a strategy can lead to bigger returns.

Strategy Laddering

Interest rates rise and fall, but in a fairly slow manner. If the economy is in a slump and interest rates are in a prolonged low-rate cycle, you do not want to get stuck buying a bunch of long-term CDs with low interest rates.

Laddering CDs can help you beat lengthy low-rate cycles because it allows you to take advantage of interest rates spread over months or years while keeping some liquidity. Laddering takes advantage of the fact that almost always, the highest interest rates are paid to the longest term CDs. In other words, a five-year CD is almost always going to have a higher rate than a one-year CD.

A CD ladder can be used for as long or as short as you would like. For this example let's use a five-year ladder with five rungs. If you have $20,000 to invest, you'd invest $4,000 in each rung. You could put $4,000 in a one-year CD, $4,000 in a two-year CD and continue up to $4,000 in a five-year CD.

After a year, the one-year CD occupying the first rung matures and each of the other CDs has one less year until maturity. In other words, the two-year CD now matures in one-year; the three-year is two years from maturity, etc. The money from the one-year CD that has just matured is rolled over into the now vacant five-year rung. Every year you're replacing the rung that's farthest out—in this case the five-year rung.

By always replacing the longest maturity, which is the top rung on the ladder, you're always reaping the benefit of earning the highest interest rates. If interest rates happen to be in a slump one year, you're only reinvesting a portion of your investment when yields are low. And you don't have to try to guess when rates are at their highest because you're constantly reinvesting.

The most important thing to keep in mind when laddering CDs: make sure the maturities correspond with your cash needs. It's no good having a one-year CD if you have an emergency halfway into the term and are in a cash crunch because your money is tied up. Penalties for early withdrawal will squash your returns. Make sure there's enough cash in your emergency fund to carry you through until the shortest rung on your ladder matures. In other words, if the first rung is a one-year CD, you need enough cash on hand for one year of living expenses.

While a five-year ladder allows you to take advantage of the best interest rates offered, however, you could make your ladder shorter if it makes you more comfortable.

The rungs should be whatever maturities suit your cash flow needs.

In an extremely low-rate environment, it's best to keep a ladder short. In that scenario, you could have a one-year ladder with rungs every three, six, nine and 12 months.

One caveat, it's not a good idea to use callable CDs in a ladder. If interest rates drop, your whole ladder, or a portion of it, could be called.

Things To Remember:

- CDs Earn higher interest rates than money market accounts
- Time-based fixed income
- Hands off investment until CD matures
- Early cash-out has interest and possible principal implications
- Interest payments may be withdrawn as they are received
- On October 3, 2008, FDIC deposit insurance temporarily increased from $100,000 to $250,000 per depositor through December 31, 2009.
- Available at banks and offline

This section was especially created to re-introduce you to the world of investing and financial independence. I'm not suggesting that you should run out and hand over all your savings to a bank and invest in CDs or go out and hire a stockbroker to invest in stocks. What I am suggesting, that you consider creating a financial growth strategy both short-term and long-term and diversify your investments, which offers you the freedom to access cash should you fall into financial hardship.

There's nothing like FINANCIAL INDEPENDENCE. You must remember, in order to secure financing with U.S. Small Business Administration or any conventional institution, there are five criteria you must meet, (1) credit worthiness, (2) collateral, (3) condition of the industry,

(4) cash flow, and (5) competency. It's unfortunate that more than 60 percent of small businesses do not meet one or more of these requirements. So what happens? The business goes into survival mode. Owners struggle, max out credit cards, over extend themselves with debt, or—worst-case scenario—dissolve.

Why take the risk—invest in your financial independence and build a portfolio you can bank on should the economy have a downturn, business slows down or a family emergency arises.

In 2003 I had a client who wanted to open a beauty salon in Los Angeles. She needed $80,000 to start the business, which included equipment and operational cost. She did not have an injection or real estate to use as collateral. I told her it would be impossible to secure capital, private or otherwise, without an injection or collateral to put up against the loan. I felt bad about the deal because I knew this was her dream. She was a single mom, living in the rural parts of Los Angeles and wanted a better life for her family. Starting a business was her way out. Just when I thought I exhausted all my resources, I decided to place one more call to an old friend who worked for an investment bank. We discussed the deal and her situation. He said if she owns any type of securities I could get her the funding she needs. I wasn't sure, so I took a stab at and asked. Low and behold, she said "I do have a 401k I've been investing in for fifteen-years and I have a five-year CD." By this time she had a well-established portfolio. Within seven days my friend, the investment banker funded her under a Securities-Based Loan for $85,000, $5,000 more than what she needed.

Today, she's thriving in her business, lives in the suburbs, provides well for her family, and to-date owns two hair salons. By her third year in business she now owns the center where she opened her first shop.

The moral of this story: invest. Nothing is impossible and everything is possible. A lender might not ask if you have investments or securities, therefore it is up to you to volunteer this information. The better prepared you are the better chance you have at getting financed.

If you haven't already noticed, I talk a lot about credit, injection, and assets, because it is so important for you to understand you can't secure financing in the traditional sense without them.

What's an Injection?
Injection is a term used interchangeably with down payment to describe the form and amount of payment a borrower must contribute toward a loan.

The injection will vary from lender to lender and can range anywhere from 10%-30%. Conventional loans and some third-party loans will require roughly 20% (unless you have an 800+ credit score); private lenders will require 12%-19% which can vary by industry type, market, and product. Poor credit and lack of collateral are top factors as to why a higher injection may be required to secure a loan.

Example: you need a loan for $240,000 to purchase an existing business. Initially you're required to put down 20%-($50,000) and the seller covers $20,000 and waives the interest for the first three years. This means the bank will only need to finance $180,000 (this is based on an informal evaluation). Ok, this sounds good, right? Now that the lender has had an opportunity to formally review all your financials, your credit and verified the equity value on your collateral (home), it turns out you have too many extended accounts and the equity on your property does not cover the loan amount; everything changes. The bank is now recommending a 1/3 split: you put down $80,000, the seller covers $80,000 and the bank will finance $80,000.

Unfortunately, this scenario happens more times than not because, borrowers don't do their homework before approaching a lender and are either denied or required to pay a larger injection to secure the loan.

Now that you have learned a little something about bonds and funds, using the table below, visit *www.bankrate.com* to compare terms and rates. Look for five institutions that offer the product of interest and compare:

CDs

- Minimum deposit
- Term/APY
- Rate

Money Market Savings Account

- Intro rate
- Number of months
- Min. open balance
- Monthly fees

Bankrate.com is a useful site to research mortgage rates, credit card rates, and loan rates. Make use of this site as you plan ahead.

CHAPTER 2

INSURANCE INVESTMENTS
or
CASH VALUE POLICIES

If you really want to play like the big boys, how about adding insurance policies to your portfolio? Did you know there are more than five different types of insurance policies on the market? Some you can actually make money with.

I am going to share two of them with you and how you can use them to your advantage.

#1 Insurance Investments: Also known as **With-profits policies.** This policy allows the policyholder to participate in the profits of the insurance company.

With-profits policies are used as a form of collective investments to achieve capital growth. Other policies offer a guaranteed return not dependent on the company's underlying investment performance; these are often referred to as *without-profit* policies which may be construed as a misnomer.

Only selected Insurance companies offer this type of policy. If you currently own a policy, call your agent to find out the specifics of owning a With-profits policy.

#2 Cash Value Policy: Cash Value policies are becoming familiar and popular financial products. They are often similar or even equal to the reserve to be held by the insurance company for the net obligations from the contract between you and the company. The amount is usually invested and earns investment income for the insurance company which is to some extent passed on to policyholders of participating contracts.

The policyholder can also use the cash value as collateral on a loan. How? When a cash value policy is purchased, like any other insurance policy you pay premiums. With this particular policy, every premium you pay is placed in an investment pool, which adds cash value to the policy. It’s more or less like putting money into a savings account, making monthly deposits and earning interest.

This is a liquid instrument you can surrender if you have accumulated enough reserves to borrow against. You are not penalized for surrendering your policy, however there are administrative fees you must pay. Check with your local insurance agent on rates and contributions. Additionally, unlike life insurance policies, you may not be required to take a health exam.

In addition to all the formentioned information on long-term investments, I want to put one more investment opportunity on the table for those of you who really want to make big dollars like the big boys. Visit www.govgex.com. Here you can buy guaranteed loans from the government on the secondary market. It requires major cash and with the right investment your return can be so much greater.

CHAPTER 3

FUNDING YOUR BUSINESS

Community Bank of Santa Clarita Valley is a prime lender for mid-to large-size businesses. The bank's interest includes Manufacturers, Import/Export and Wholesalers.

When making a lending decision, Cal Naulls, First Vice President-Regional Manager, looks for a consistent, increase in both sales and profits over a three-year period of time; confident management; and a strong business industry.

Community Bank of Santa Clarita Valley approves more than twenty-three loans to local businesses each quarter, almost 100 such loans a year.

We talked about bonds, notes, TIPS, and certificates of deposit, long-term investment opportunities and securities in the previous section. Now let's switch our focus to financial institutions and their benefactors. In this section you will learn about lenders, loan programs, and alternative financing options.

Types of Lenders

There are two types of lenders: **Institutional** ***and Non-Institutional.***

Each offers financing in specific areas and has specialized programs to suit one or multiple markets. They differ in loan-qualification criteria and how much financing is distributed to a borrower. Be sure and exercise due diligence, research the different types of products offered, interest rates, approval ratio for your industry and qualifications.

Lenders can be very judgmental when it comes to a client's preparedness and organization. So be prepared to speak their language and have all your ducks lined up in a row. Institutional lenders are conventional lenders, savings banks, commercial banks, mutual savings banks, credit unions and insurance companies.

We'll review those that are most pertinent in achieving your financial goal.

Conventional Lenders: These are the financial institutions you would first think of when borrowing money, and are preferred institutions, which operate in the private banking sector. They perform independently, therefore are not bound by government regulations in terms of credit policies for their borrowers. Most of these lenders receive guaranteed funds from the Small Business Administration (SBA) which funnels billions of dollars to financial institutions thus making more lending opportunities available to the small business community.

The SBA plays a vital role in the financing industry. If a borrower meets the requirements, SBA will guarantee up to 85% of the loan.

Some Conventional Lenders are:

1.Wells Fargo

2. Community Bank

3. Mission Valley Bank

4. Bank of America

5. U.S. Bank

6. Citi Bank

Commercial Lenders: ***These*** are the most versatile of all lenders. They make home loans, equity loans, business loans and other short-term loans. Commercial banks manage consumer checking and savings accounts and certificates of deposit. Using those funds and other resources borrowed from other intermediaries, commercial banks make loans to investment buyers, builders and businesses. They are the largest originators of commercial real estate loans for acquisitions, development and construction of real estate projects.

Commercial lenders vary in project interest and geographical locations. As with conventional lenders, the application process can be time consuming and involves a great deal of paper work.

Funding Matrix (will vary):

Real Estate:

- Units & Single Family Residences
- Churches
- Garage Conversions
- Warehouses

Commercial:

- Office Condos
- Condo Conversions
- Medical Condos
- Gas Stations
- Grocery Stores
- Public Facilities (school, library, community center)
- Mixed use
- Acquisitions

Other:

- Receivables
- Refinances
- Bridge Loans

Lending Parameters:

- Loan Amounts range from $100,000 - $300 Million
- 65%-85% Loan to Value (LTV)
- Fully Stated No Doc Loans
- Credit Score 640+
- Competitive Rates

Mutual Savings Banks: These are banks, which allow their depositors to share in the profits after all formal expenses, reserves and contributions to the surplus have been made. Therefore, the depositors not only make money from their deposits, they also draw interest on all funds the bank handles. Mutual Savings Banks are not common in California.

In section two, I discussed a couple of insurance policies and the strategic advantage you could have with them. Now let's talk about insurance companies as lenders.

Insurance Companies: These are traditional lenders, which provide financing to the real estate industry. They will finance property acquisitions, developers building multiple properties or commercial properties that require high dollar loans or investments.

Non-Institutional Lenders

Non-Institutional lenders are indirect lenders acting as agents on behalf of institutional lenders to satisfy funding for borrowers. They include Certified Development Companies, CEDLI, Valley economic Development Center Centers, private investors, and independent organizations.

Certified Development Companies: They will originate a loan, which can be a tremendous help to borrowers looking for LTVs at 75% or more. A CDC will take a second position on a loan at 10%-15% to make up the entire loan amount.

Many third-party lenders will offer guarantee programs through SBA and are small-business friendly.

(CEDLI) Co-Lending for Small Businesses

CEDLI provides capital in both urban and rural areas to growing businesses that are currently not able to qualify for conventional bank financing. All small businesses in all industries are eligible for financing. Providing access to women and minority-owned businesses is a high priority. CEDLI works in partnership with its member banks in the Co-Lending Program by funding up to 50% of the loan requirement of a business in the form of subordinated debt, while a member bank funds the other 50% or more of the financing need. CEDLI is a great funding source for childcare services.

Angel Investors: These are individuals, groups or organizations that provide private financing to businesses. They also can provide both money and management expertise. Angels invest in 60% of startup companies, investing five times more money than venture capitalists.

Advantages:

- No credit checks. Also will invest based on the type of business and its potential.
- Will provide management support.
- Will bring experience to the operations and development of the business.

Disadvantages:

- Higher interest rate than a bank.
- Take control of the business.
- Take large interest in the business stakes.

Investor Resources:

1. www.Go Big Network.com
2. www.Investors Garage.com
3. www.BEDZZ INN.com
4. www.Breadstreet.com
5. www.lava.org
6. www.techcoastangels.com
7. www.prosperloanmarketplace.com
8. www.kiva.org
9. www.microplace.com
10. Women's World Banking

Private Lending Organizations: These provide in-house financing to borrowers. They are self-funding organizations not associated with SBA or conventional institutions. Their rates are sometimes lower than conventional lenders and have fewer restrictions. This is an ideal funding source for start-ups, because they are community-driven and contribute to the development of emerging community businesses.

1. Jewish Free Loan Association (www.jfla.org)

2. Accion (www.accion.com)

What Lenders Look For in an Ideal Borrower

Lenders will analyze the past and present trends of a business including its performance and the credit history of all principal owners. The business will be compared to other businesses in its industry and those, which operate at the same level. Insufficient cash flow, poor credit scores and debt to income ratios are also underlying factors.

LaKisha Gant, a Loan Officer for many years with a CDC small business finance company, works closely with many lenders and told me first hand—lenders want to know you and understand your capital needs; you must have positive financial projections; have a succession plan; and more importantly, lenders want to know you have the ability to pay back the debt.

Bankers will evaluate your loan request using the "five Cs of credit"

1. Character--Are you trust worthy? Do you have?
   - A credit score of at least 600 (will vary by lender)?
   - Any current collections (within six months)?
   - Liens or judgments?
   - A bankruptcy within five years?
   - Student loans in default?

2. Capacity—What are your financial strengths and track record?
   - If you've been in business for a period of time, do you have a positive cash flow trend?
   - If you are a start-up, do you project a positive cash flow trend of at least 20% each year?
   - Does your business have adequate equity?
   - Can you pay back the loan?
   - Do you have a substantial amount of outflow?*

3. Capital-- How much of your own money do you have invested in the business? How much:
   - Did you contribute to the development of the business?
   - Did or can you invest in the business (start ups)?
   - Do you have in your bank account?
   - Money can you put toward the loan injection?

4. Collateral--What assets do you have to support the primary source of repayment?
   - Do you have property?
   - How much is your property worth?
   - Does the property have sufficient equity?

5. Conditions---How is the business affected by the industry and economic changes?
   - Is your business type in demand?
   - What is the status of your industry?
   - Is your product/service marketable?

In addition to the 5 Cs, lenders look for sufficient cash flow to service existing and new debt and positive operating trends for three years.

What SBA Looks For In A Proposal:

- Ability to repay the loan on time from the projected operating cash flow.
- Owners and operators who are of good character.
- Feasible business plan.
- Management expertise and commitment necessary for success.
- Sufficient funds, including the SBA-guaranteed loan, to operate the business on a sound financial basis.
- For new businesses, sufficient funds, which includes the resources to meet start-up expenses and the initial operating phase.
- Adequate equity invested in the business.

Sufficient collateral to secure the loan or all available collateral if the loan cannot be fully secured.

CHAPTER 4

LOAN PROGRAMS

FINANCING OPTIONS

Community Bank of Santa Clarita Valley provides Conventional Buyers' Loans (Working Capital- Lines of Credit), Equipment Term Loans, Commercial Owner-Occupied Real Estate Loans and Letters of Credit.

Loan Programs

SBA:

- Community Express

The Community Express Loan Program provides streamlined business financing and management and technical assistance to small businesses located in distressed or underserved markets. Loans are available from $5,000 to $250,000. (Vary according to Preferred Lender)

Note: For Community Express loans of $25,000 or less a lender may ask a borrower to use SBA's online T/A (Technical Assistance). The required pre-loan technical assistance prescribed by the Customized Training Plan must be completed before the loan is disbursed.

- Patriot Express

The Patriot Express Initiative combines a pilot loan initiative with SBA's traditional small business ownership training for veterans and military community members wanting to establish or expand small businesses. Loans are available up to $500,000.

- SBA Express

SBA Express is available to lenders to obtain a guarantee on small loans up to $350,000. SBA will guarantee up to 50 percent of an SBA Express loan. Loans under $25,000 do not require collateral.

- 7 (a) Loan Program

The 7 (a) Loan Program is the most flexible of SBA's lending programs. Eligibility is based on four different factors and the business must qualify as a small business.

1. Size
2. Nature of business
3. Use of proceeds
4. Miscellaneous factors such as SBA credit from other institutions, use of personal assets, and principal ownership use of resources.

- CAP Lines

This is a specialized umbrella loan program designed to help small businesses meet their short-term and cyclical working-capital needs.

CAP Lines can be used to finance seasonal working-capital needs; finance the direct costs of performing certain construction, service and supply contracts; finance the direct cost associated with commercial and residential construction performed on a speculative basis; finance operating capital by obtaining advances against existing inventory and accounts receivable; and consolidate short-term debt.

Note: Check with your local SBA office to find a lender that supports CAP Programs.

The five programs under the CAP Lines umbrella:

1. The Contract Loan Program (Finance material and labor needs for contracts)
2. The Seasonal Line of Credit Program (Finance short-term, seasonal increases of accounts receivable and inventory)
3. The Builders Line Program (Financing for small general contractors involved in residential or commercial construction or building rehabilitation for re-sale)
4. The Small Asset-Based Line (For revolving lines up to $200,000 to purchase inventory, pay direct labor, finance accounts receivable, advanced against existing inventory)
5. The Standard Asset-Based Line (Same as the SABL, but used for loan amounts over $200,000)

- Certified Development Company Loans (CDC) (504 Loan Program)

The 504 Loan Program is an economic development program that provides long-term, fixed rate, subordinate mortgage financing for acquisition and/or renovation of capital assets including land, buildings and equipment. A 10 percent injection is required for existing businesses two years old or more and a 15 to 20 percent injection is required for all start-ups under 2 years old.

Lending Matrix for 7a and 504 loans:

- Working Capital (7a)
  Can be used for:
    1. Payroll
    2. Storefront improvement
    3. Purchasing inventory
    4. Marketing
    5. Purchasing small equipment

- Equipment Purchase (7a/504)
    1. Purchase large machinery
    2. Purchase mass equipment

- Construction (504)
    1. Building
    2. Remodeling

- Real Estate (504)
    1. Purchase commercial property
    2. Purchase another business

I also want to introduce you to a couple more SBA loan programs. The SBA's Investment Program, known as SBIC and the Rural Business Investment Program.

SBIC: In 1958 Congress created The Small Business Investment Company (SBIC) program. SBICs, licensed by the Small Business Administration, are privately owned and managed investment firms. They are participants in a vital partnership between government and the private sector economy. With the private capital they raise and with funds borrowed at favorable rates through SBA, SBICs provide financing in the form of debt or equity to small businesses. Visit www.sba.gov/inv to learn more about this program and find an SBIC partner in your area.

Rural Business Investment Program (RBIP): RBIP is a joint initiative between the U. S. Department of Agriculture (USDA) and the Small Business Administration.

The RBIP was created to promote economic development and job creation in rural areas. RBICs must identify targeted Rural Areas and demonstrate how they will assist those areas through disciplined, profit-oriented investing in rural enterprises and through hands-on technical assistance to rural enterprises via Operational Assistance (OA) grant funding.

Additionally, RBICs must address the following requirements:

- At least 75% of RBIC investments measured both by dollars invested and number of loans must be made in Rural Business Concerns (i.e., an enterprise whose principal office is located outside a standard metropolitan statistical area or within a community with a population of 50,000 or fewer).

- No more than 10% of investments measured both by number and dollars invested may be in enterprises whose principal office is located in an urban area (defined by the Census as having a population of 150,000 or more.)

- At least 50% of RBIC investments (measured both by number and dollars invested) must be in "Smaller Enterprises," and of those, at least 50% must be in "Small Business Concerns".

Targeted Rural Areas: Kentucky, Tennessee, Ohio, West Virginia, Virginia, North Carolina, South Carolina, Georgia, Alabama, Mississippi and Arkansas.

You can contact your local Small Business Administration office to inquire about these programs in your home state.

Collateralized Loans

Let's say you go to a lender looking for $50,000 to start a printing business or you are a manufacturer and want to expand and you don't have the down payment. What you do own are large pieces of machinery and equipment. If you own the machinery or equipment (not leased), you can get financed under a collateralized loan up to appraised value. In essence, you are putting the machinery and equipment up as collateral.

Financing Options

Lines of Credit

Can be financed up to two years and can be used for working capital, storefront improvement, inventory, etc. When securing a line of credit, funds are not made available to you at once, funds are distributed on an as needed basis.

***Term Loans*:** Will vary.

Real Estate loans:	10-25
Business Acquisition:	10 years
Equipment:	10 years
Working Capital:	2 to 7 years

Credit Card Receivable Financing

Need an immediate infusion of capital for an unexpected repair bill or to take advantage of a new business opportunity? Smart, simple business financing is available from $5,000 to $350,000 (or higher) in 7-10 business days based only on your credit card sales volume. (Max. funding is from 3/4 to 2 times your average. monthly credit card sales.)

It requires no collateral, assets, or high credit scores if the business owner has been in business a year with at least $3,000 of credit card sales per month.

Advantage:

- Can get quick cash

Disadvantage:

- Must give lender up to 15% of all receipt transactions
- Money is taken at the end of the month
- Will pay back more than 5% of loan than with other lenders

Accounts Receivable

What is Accounts Receivable (Factoring) Financing?

Accounts receivable financing (A/R financing), which is also known as factoring, is the conversion of a company's business accounts receivable (invoices) into immediate cash by selling those invoices at a discount. A/R financing is not a loan. There is no interest nor principal to repay.

Financing accounts receivable has become the preferred financial tool in obtaining flexible working capital for businesses of all sizes. The receivable credit line is determined by the financial strength of the customer (buyer), not the client (the seller of the receivables).

Advantages: Strengthen your business

- **Pass off Collections:** Outsourcing your accounts receivable management to another company frees up your resources to focus on other more productive activities such as selling.

- **Free up Working Capital:** Accounts receivable funding allows a company to free up capital tied up in inventory.

- **Quick Financing:** Accounts receivable factoring will not require a business plan or tax statements. It's a quick form of cash often used for businesses experiencing a cash crunch.

Strengthens your credit

A/R financing creates no debt. So, unlike a loan, it will not show up on your balance sheet as a liability, it's "off-balance sheet" financing. You'll increase cash and decrease accounts receivable thus strengthening your financial statements.

A/R financing vs. bank financing

- A/R financing is based only on your accounts receivable and on the financial strength and stability of your business customers, not the credit worthiness of your own business. So even if you're a new business or you have a less-than-stellar business credit rating, you can still be eligible for A/R financing, which cannot be said for bank financing. A/R funding sources (or Factors) often welcome clients that banks turn away.

- It offers a dependable, continuing source of cash without the necessity of making separate loan applications. It provides continual cash flow without the requirement of periodic payments or interim payoffs for bank financing.

- Gives a business-increased access to cash as sales and receivables increase. There is no ceiling beyond which the factor must stop providing cash. The more sales a business makes, the more cash it can draw. The Factor does not concentrate on the business' debt-to-equity ratio to provide funds as banks do.

- And as A/R financing strengthens the credit of your business, you may then be eligible for bank loans and credit lines in the future.

A/R financing vs. Equity financing
You do not need to give up any equity or ownership in your business by seeking outside investments. You retain full control over your business.

Processing

1. A two-page application
2. An accounts receivable aging report
3. Submit a customer list with credit limit
4. Copy of articles of Incorporation or DBA filing
5. Purchase orders or rate confirmation agreements
6. Invoices to factor

Qualifications for Receivable Financing

Alternative financing options are suitable for companies with seasonal or uneven sales patterns or start-up operations with no financial base to rely upon. Any business can qualify for receivable financing if it generates sales on open credit terms to customers with financial credit strength.

"A prospect must have Accounts Receivable (A/R) total of $1MM (Million) plus, which 80% of the totals would be advanced, minus the ARs 90 days past due."

-Cal Naulls, *Community Bank of Santa Clarita Valley.*

Stated-No-Doc Financing

You don't hear much about stated-no-doc financing anymore. Very few lenders offer this as a financing option. An institutional lender would not offer this option. Private lenders are more likely to take the risk of lending money based on how much money you have in the bank and the net worth of the investment. Depending on the investor, it can take as little as one week to receive funding and the money does not have to be seasoned. (For those of you unfamiliar with the term seasoned, I am referring to the number of days the money must sit in a bank account prior to funding.)

Requirements (Will vary by lender):

Commercial Projects:

- Owner user stated income up to 75% loan to value
- Programs include 3/1 ARM, 5/1 ARM
- 15 yr fixed or 30 year fixed
- Minimum fico score 650
- Multi-Family (5+ units) or 3-4 units in restricted markets
- Retail (shopping center/strip malls, office, light industrial)
- 3 months bank statements to prove you have a steady flow of income.
- 20% to 30% injection/down payment.

Stated Income Residential

- Minimum fico score 680
- Minimum 3 months reserves
- Asset based lending (Will vary by lender)

Securities Based Lending

Need quick cash? This is the ideal lending structure, and it only works if you have **SECURITIES** to use as collateral.

Protect Your Stock Portfolio AND Get Cash. A securities-based loan program allows you to leverage your securities portfolio and offers you protection from market decline without selling your securities.

No Credit Review Required. Since the loan is securities-based, there are no credit or income requirements. In addition, the program allows you to continue to reap the rewards of any appreciation and dividends generated by the pledged securities.

Eligible securities include stocks, bonds, penny stocks, mutual funds, and foreign exchanges.

Program details:

- No Credit Requirements.
- Fixed rates between 3%-5%.
- Terms: From 3 to 10 years.
- LTV: From 35% to 80% of value of asset.
- Non-Recourse: You can walk away anytime.
- It is a loan, not a sale.

The program is very flexible. At the end of the term, the loan can be paid off, refinanced, or renewed. You keep all market appreciation and dividends.

Just another reason why owning mutual funds, bonds, and stocks is so important to a business. At anytime if you're cash strapped, you will always have a portfolio you can count on.

Most Insurance and Investment companies offer this program. Requirements may differ, so be sure to confirm, compare, and ask questions about the program's structure.

To secure hard money costs more than soft money. This brand of funding should be the last resort and only pursued when a borrower doesn't qualify for a SBA or conventional loan. Keep in mind interest rates are higher and investors expect a more lucrative Return On Investment (ROI). Nevertheless, there are fewer restrictions and the loan can fund in less time. Hard money is a good option for borrowers with challenging credit.

Finding hard money can be a challenge. It's all in whom you know. Start networking with financial advisors, CPA's, call around or google investment banks, and brokerage companies. Insurance companies are also good resources. You may also want to rub a few elbows with realtors: they too have access to commercial lenders.

Hard money is ideal for development projects, large acquisitions, and debt or equity financing. You can also borrow capital to refinance property. If you own improved land it can be used to secure financing or borrow funds to improve it. Also, keep in mind, these investors won't fund deals under a million dollars: you must be cash flow positive, have assets (preferably real estate with equity), and have a good track record.

When searching for hard money, a few things to look out for:

(1) never pay anyone upfront: closing cost-fees should be covered upon funding

(2) be sure to read all agreements thoroughly; and

(3) do your due diligence and research the company.

There are many scams out there, don't get caught up.

If someone requests a non-refundable fee in excess of $5,000 or more upfront---**RUN.**

CHAPTER 5

PUTTING YOUR DUCKS IN A ROW

5.1
How to Become Bankable

1. Positive flow of cash:

There are two documents lenders (conventional and non-conventional) pay close attention to: profit and loss statement and the balance sheet. Both documents will tell the whole financial story of your business. They will tell the lender if you're a high risk, medium risk, or low risk candidate for financing. Profit and loss statements reflect your cash flow trends, positive and negative. Lenders look for the bottom line numbers, which should be in black demonstrating break-even or profit.

For new businesses it's important to plan and project realistic cash flow trends, month-to-month for a period of three years out. This demonstrates to a lender: 1) you've done your homework, 2) projections were well thought out, and 3) your potential profitability. Note, some lenders are cautious about financing cash flow projections. They would prefer to see some history of cash flows, incoming and outgoing.

Existing businesses: a lender looks for cash flow management and evaluates the business based on its previous cash flow history. The previous three years determine your risk and future projections determine your probability to carry on the business. If for some reason previous statements show negative trends, be prepared to demonstrate how you intend to improve sales and generate a positive flow of cash. This can be done by creating a well-thought-out marketing plan along with projected statements to support it.

2. Income stability: Lenders want to make sure their money is well invested. Personal income plays a large role in their decision to fund your business. There must be an influx of cash available to the business in the event revenue from sales is low. This is where your personal income comes into play. It should exceed 30% or more of your expenses to cover monthly fixed and variable costs. You must also be able to show your ability to repay the note during times of uncertainty, from personal income.

3. Have valued assets (personal and business)?

Bankers favor businesses with minimum levels of cash, accounts receivable, inventory, and other current assets on hand to cover slow periods. Additionally, these assets are liquid—if the business fails, the bank can recover part or all of its investment.

Personal assets with value and are liquid can be all the leverage you need to secure a loan. As previously mentioned in section 1—stocks, bonds, funds and alternative securities are all valuable assets to bargain with.

4. The 5 C's:

Credit: Are you credit worthy.

- Should have a credit score of at least 600
- Don't have any current collections (within 6 months)
- No liens or judgments
- No bankruptcy's within 5 years
- Not default student loans

Capacity: What are your financial strengths and track record.

- If you've been in business for a period of time, do you have a positive cash flow trend
- Start-ups, does your projections project a positive cash flow trend of at least 20% each year
- Does your business have adequate equity
- Can you pay back the loan
- Do you have a substantial amount of outflow

Condition: How is the business affected by the industry and economy changes.

- Is your business type in demand
- What is the status of your industry
- Is your product/service marketable

Capital: How much of your own money do you have invested in the business and can you.

- How much did you contribute to the development of the business
- How much money did invest
- How much money do you have in you bank account

Cash flow: What are your financial strengths and track record.

- If you've been in business for a period of time, do you have a positive cash flow trend.
- Start-ups, does your projections project a positive cash flow trend of at least 20% each year.
- Does your business have adequate equity.

- Can you pay back the loan
- Do you have a substantial amount of outflow

The 5 C's are criteria's lenders use to evaluate a borrower's worthiness and to determine if they are a likely candidate for funding.

5. Working Capital Cushion:

Lenders would prefer to see more working capital than less. This is a good sign of increasing financial health. There are two conditions which a lender analyzes to determine the probability of repayment for a working capital loan: (1) *timing* of payments and (2) *value* of the current assets.

Example: timing: the bank approves a short-term loan for $200,000 and the loan is due in 90 days. The business has accounts payable and accrued expenses of $100,000, which are due in 30 days. If the business has only $300,000 in current assets, its working capital, including the bank loan, is zero. Timing reflects when accounts receivable will convert to cash to repay the loan. It is important to have a sufficient amount of working capital to cover the amount of shrinkage in the value of the assets.

6. Reduce Credit

Most borrowers believe more credit is better than little or no credit. That's not true. You can have the perfect credit score, bills current and have money in the bank. But a lender may view too much credit as a high risk if you are extended. When I say extended I mean over extended with credit. You have reached your credit capacity, which exceeds your income ratio. (Income ratio will vary and is measured by income to debt)

I had a client with an AAA credit score, never late on his payments and he had more than enough money to put towards the loan. He also had four rental properties, had recently bought a $900,000 home, and his wife bought a new truck. As if this wasn't impressive, he worked for a fortune-500 company making a six-figure salary and his wife was a lawyer.

His goal was to retire from his job, open a retail store and hopefully build a chain. Well, there were a few problems: He had no equity to pull from, his rental properties were financed at 100% with no down-payment and his home had been purchased six months prior. Remember both he and his wife had good incomes. However because their combined income only exceeded 10% of their expenses and not the required 30% they were extended and denied.

So, if you are extended in credit, try to pay off some of the debt and pay down any fixed monthly costs/payments.

5.2

FINANCIAL PROJECTIONS

Projecting Your Financials

Why am I discussing financial projections? These are other factors, which a lender---institutional or non-institutional--will want to see to determine if you are a profitable company. Besides, every business owner should know, have, and interpret financial projections.

Income Statement:

12-Month sales forecasts are used to determine the value and number of sales per product item or services, needed to generate a significant amount of profit and meet your financial goals. A sales forecast is very important to the outcome of the business's profit margin when creating a Profit & Loss (P&L) statement. Always use realistic numbers when completing this section. If the numbers are projected beyond your capacity, you may run the risk of not meeting your financial goals and fall in the **RED.**

Profit & Loss Projections:

12-month P&Ls are designed to help the business owner identify projected profits or losses within a year. This form also assumes the probability of increasing or decreasing specific areas associated with revenues, cost of sales or expenses that may affect the outcome of the business's annual operations need.

A P&L is where information from the sales forecast is transferred, which balance out your income and outflow to project a gross profit. After developing your P&L you may discover areas where some adjustments should be made to ensure the company shows growth by an increased margin base to earn a profit. (**Note:** Each year should reflect a 20% marginal increase at minimum.)

- Your projections will come from a forecast of sales, cost of goods sold, expenses, and profit month-by-month for one year.
- Profit projections should be accompanied by a narrative explaining the major assumptions used to estimate company income and expenses.

  - **Cost of Goods Sold** ***(also called Cost of Sales or COGS):*** COGS are those expenses directly related to producing or buying your products or services. For example, purchases of inventory or raw materials, as well as the wages (and payroll taxes) of employees directly involved in producing your products/services.

- **Gross Profit***:* Gross Profit is Total Sales minus Total COGS. In the "%" columns, the spreadsheet will show Gross Profit as a % of Total Sales.

- **Operating Expenses** ***(also called Overhead):*** These are necessary expenses, which, are not directly related to making or buying your products/services. Rent, utilities, telephone, interest, and the salaries (and payroll taxes) of office and management employees are examples.

- **Net Profit***:* The spreadsheet will subtract Total Operating Expenses from Gross Profit to calculate Net Profit. In the "%" columns, it will show Net Profit as a % of Total Sales.

Four-Year Projection:
Four-Year Projection is a long-term forecast over a period of years, which enables the business owner to foresee the financial future of the business. This projection is a manifestation of the Profit & Loss sheet with four years of planning.

Balance Sheet:
A balance sheet is one of the fundamental financial reports used for reporting and demonstrating the financial strength of the business. Additionally, a balance sheet shows what items of value are held by the company (assets), and what its debts are (liabilities). When liabilities are subtracted from assets, the remainder is owners' equity. A lender is most interested in seeing a balance sheet when determining the business's ability to produce financial stability and profitability.

Break-Even Analysis:
A break-even analysis predicts the sales volume, at a given price, required to recover total costs. In other words, it's the sales level, which is the dividing line between operating at a loss and operating at a profit.

(The Break-even Formula: Break-even sales = Fixed Costs - Variable Cost)

Fixed costs are those that remain the same regardless of your sales volume. They are expressed in dollars; for example: Rent, insurance and real estate taxes.

Variable costs are those, which change as your volume of business changes. They are expressed as a percent of sales such as: inventory, raw materials and direct production labor.

Fixed	**13,000**	**13,000**	
Price – Cost	**\$20 - \$8 = \$12**	**\$12**	**= 1,083**
(Retail Cost--Cost to produce)			**(Units Sold Mthly)**

This is an example of a break-even analysis for 1 unit/product

5.3

Preparing Your Letter of Request

Getting the loan is a matter of good salesmanship. Don't assume the banker knows everything about your business. It is your job to educate him or her. The first step is to prepare a ***loan proposal*** containing the following:

Note: If you are a start-up you will require a full business plan including three years financial projections. For existing businesses of two years or more, an executive summary will be sufficient.

1. Loan Request:

Purpose of Loan
Amount Required
Term Desired
Source of Repayment
Collateral Available

Example: JP Anderson & Holts requests a five-year term loan of $200,000, secured by inventory valued at $800,000, for the purpose of purchasing additional inventory due to sales increases. Repayment will be primarily from net profits and secondarily from liquidation of collateral and guarantees, if necessary.

It is also anticipated that short-term borrowings for seasonal needs will be required in the amount of $300,000. This loan will be repaid out of cash flow and will be secured by assigned accounts receivable of at least $100,000.

2. History & Nature of the Business: A general overview of the business.

Brief and to the point, one or two paragraphs describing your business.

Example: Jp Anderson & Holts was founded as a sole proprietorship by its current owner in 2000 as a Grant-writing agency servicing non-profit organizations. The company was incorporated in 2006 and the common stock is currently owned by Ms. C. Riley 100%.

The Company is located at 25543 Sierra Rampart Ste. 138 in Santa Jose, CA. The company has shown substantial progress and has had to move three times to expand its capabilities. During the past three years, sales have tripled.

3. Management: Brief résumés on all officers, directors, owners and key personnel, including age, health, salary, business experience, business affiliations, education, experience in the area pertaining to the business, time to be devoted to the business, and degree of ownership of the business.

Age, Experience, Education of each owner/partner
Other key advisors

Example: Claudette Riley, President and 100% owner, age 39, good health. Salary-- $60,000 plus bonus. New York University graduate and currently attending Pepperdine University--- Doctorate Degree. Business experience includes four years in management, two years in human resource and six years as a business consultant. Member of NAFE, ABWA and API.

4. General Information: Employment: The total number of employees and a description of the critical skills required. Description of labor relations, including any prior difficulties and a summary of any current union contracts.

Products: Products sold and services rendered, and the relative importance of each principal product or service to the volume of the business.

Market Area and Method of Distribution, Customers & Marketing: The type, number, location and financial strength of customers, including the names of the five largest, and the percentage of the gross revenue accounted for by these customers. A description of the techniques used to create the demand for the product/service.

Major Customers- *Example: the company is a consulting and service company, providing business solutions to entrepreneurs, small business owners and agencies servicing them. Primary customers consist of entrepreneurs and small businesses. Customers total 200-300, with 20- 30 customers accounting for 30% of the business. No one customer is key. Advertising expense is minimal. Exclusively working for Small Business Development Centers and Educational institutions and three other associations, and in this capacity provides service to other agencies servicing small businesses in California. Primary aspect of the business is service--- the ability to have products and resources available for customers when needed.*

Suppliers--- Sources of Supply: Brief description of the significant materials and supplies used, including adequacy of the resources, names of the major suppliers and adequacy of available storage and facilities.

Competition---A summary of the competitive conditions in the industry, including a list of the largest competitors.

Facilities---A detailed description of the real and physical property and equipment, including age, condition, insurance coverage and adaptability to the principal business in which engaged. Include a summary of agreements pertaining to any encumbrances on property or equipment owned, or lease or rental agreements on non-owned property.

5. Financial Information:

- Three years Balance Sheet
- Most recent three years financial statements and tax returns
- Ratio analysis with appropriate comments
- Personal financial statement (dated within 90 days of the loan request)
- Income statement (for at least one year)
- Cash budget
- Comprehensive cash flow analysis

5.4

BUILDING A FUNDING STRATEGY

To create a good strategy you will need to cross reference information from various sections in this book. This strategy is used for the purpose of identifying the proper financing most suitable for your business needs and to determine if your business is bankable.

First: you must conduct an income evaluation to determine how much money you have or will have available and if it's enough to meet the financial criteria of the loan.

1. List annual sources of income. (e.g. salary, rental income, interest)

2. List annual fixed expenses. (e.g. household, maintenance, mortgage)

3. Total annual income and expenses separately.

4. Multiply total expenses by 30% and add the two figures (this will be the amount of income required to meet the standard income test).

5. Now that you know how much income is required, subtract expenses from your income.

The purpose of this evaluation is to make sure the borrower can maintain their household needs and cover the monthly note.

Example:
Total income: $100,000
Total expenses: $50,000 (Multiplied by 30% = $15,000)

$50,000 + $15,000 = $65,000 (required income)

Income: $100,000
Expenses: — $50,000

Total Available Income: $50,000 (20% more than required)
Borrower may qualify for a business loan.

Note: Visit www.wadeinstitute.org for a copy of the actual worksheet to perform this evaluation, under forms.

Second: you must determine how much capital is required to start the business. One mistake most business owners make when applying for capital: they ask for too much or too little.

1. Make a list of items needed to start the business (e.g. equipment, improvements, fixtures, hardware) and the cost for each item.

2. Total these start-up costs.

3. List monthly business operational expenses (e.g. rent, supplies, labor) and total them.

4. List and total your monthly personal expenses.

5. Combine your monthly business expense and personal expense and multiply this total by three months. Add your start-up costs from step 2. This will be the projected amount of financing you will need to start the business.

Lenders will provide you with three months of operational support and funds for start-up expenses. However, you must demonstrate to the lender how you plan to continue business thereafter. Your personal income and wages are also factors. If the income is not enough to cover both personal and business expenses, funding from an institutional lender may not be an option.

How do you determine which is the best strategy to use for accessing capital?

Use the following graph as a guide to determine the best strategy for accessing capital. Refer back to the beginning sections, to determine which loan program, financing options, and lender best suits your business and financial needs.

Example	**Operational**	**Acquisitions**	**Real Estate**	**Inventory**
Need	Working Capital	Purchase New Business	Purchase New Building	Purchase New Equipment
Loan Amount	$$5,000	$250,000	$2 Million	$200,000
Loan Type	Community Express	504	504	7a
Lender	Third Party VDEC	CDC	CDC	Citi Bank
Credit History	Fair-630	Excellent-760	Excellent-760	Good 720
Net Income	$3,000	$50,000	$80,000	$75,000
Monthly Installment	$145	$2,293	$17,000	$2,267
Maturity	18	120	120	120
Interest Rate	$3,150@3.5%	$18,000@3%	$6M @3%	$72,000@3%
Total Loan	$8,150	$268,000	$206M	$272,000

To determine the approximate monthly repayment amount use the following calculations: Amount of loan ($250,000) multiplied by interest rate (4%) divided by number of years (months) 5 years = 60 months.

CHAPTER 6

DEALING WITH LENDERS

How to Deal with a Banker

Bankers are trained to always require two sources of repayment. Some form of collateral (accounts receivable, inventory, or a mortgage on fixed assets) should back up the primary source, cash flow for short-term loans and earnings for long-term loans. Should something go wrong with the original plan, the banker always has at least one fallback position.

They will usually require a personal guarantee from the owner of the business. Why? Because they want your psychological commitment and know you are committed to the success of the business. Bankers don't necessarily expect to gain a lot of financial security from your personal signature, but they want to ensure they have your total support and dedication to making the business successful.

Negotiating with a Lender

You can negotiate with a lender. If you have good credit, no collections and can pay the required injection, you can ask the lender to reduce your interest rate. Typically interest rates include market value plus prime. The market value is the government rate of 2%, and prime is the lenders' rate of charge, which can be anywhere from 3% to 6%, giving you an overall APR of 5% to 9%.

It's always worth asking; a closed mouth never gets fed. Go for it!

You can also negotiate a term. For instance, you need a line of credit or working capital and the term of the loan is 12 months. If you know you will need more than 12 months, ask for a longer term. At the lender's discretion, they can extend the term. Why would a lender do this? They want your business; if you are a good candidate and meet all the requirements, the underwriter will do whatever he/she can to accommodate the borrower and ensure the deal is beneficial to both parties.

What You Should Know Before Meeting A Lender

Uniform Commercial Code (UCC) Filing

A UCC Filing is a security blanket for lenders. It allows the lender to place a lien on the business property to secure a large loan request in the event the borrower does not have a sufficient injection. A filing can also be requested if the borrower is flagged as a medium to high risk. Not all, but most lenders require a UCC Filing.

There are occasions when a lender may not require a UCC Filing such as when the borrower is able to provide a large down-payment toward the loan or has been in business for a number of years and shows profit stability and/or growth.

Know that, during your reporting periods, if the lender notices your revenue has decreased, there is no equity in the business, and payments are not being made as required, being the account holder, the lender can take hold of any property used as part of the UCC to cover any outstanding funds owed against the loan.

Percentage of Guarantees
The SBA only guarantees a portion of any particular loan. Each loan will also have an un-guaranteed portion giving the lender a certain amount of exposure to risk.

For 7 (a) loans of $150,000 or less the SBA will guarantee as much as 85 percent and for loans over $150,000 up to 75 percent. The maximum loan amount to any one business is $1.5 million.

Interest Rates and Fees
Both fixed and variable interest rates are available. Rates are set based on the lowest prime rate and maturity. For loans with maturities of less than seven years the rate will be fixed or start at prime plus no more than 2.25 percent. For loans with maturities of seven years or more the rate can be prime plus 2.25 percent. For loans under $50,000 and loans processed through SBA Express, rates are permitted to be higher.

Note: The SBA charges the lender a nominal upfront fee to provide its guaranty and the lender may pass the charge on to you.

7(a) Loan Maturities
Loan maturities are based on the ability to repay the loan, the purpose of the loan proceeds and the useful life of the assets financed.

Structure
Most loans are repaid with monthly payments of principal and interest. Borrowers can request that the lender establish the loan with interest-only payments during the start-up and expansion phases to allow the business time to generate the income to start repaying the loan. There are no balloon payments or call provisions allowed on any 7 (a) loan. The lender may not charge a prepayment penalty if the loan is paid off before maturity, but the SBA will charge the borrower a prepayment fee if the loan has a maturity of 15 or more years and is pre-paid during the first three years.

Collateral
SBA expects every loan to be fully secured, however SBA will not decline a request to guaranty a loan if the only unfavorable factor is insufficient collateral. Every SBA loan is to be secured by all available assets (both business and personal) until the recovery value equals the loan amount or until assets have been applied to the extent that they are reasonably available, to adequately secure the loan. Personal guaranties are required from all the principal owners of the business. Liens on personal assets of the principals may be required (a UCC filing).

Do's and Don'ts

Do:

- Make an appointment and allocate enough time.
- Talk straight, tell the good and bad. Failing to discuss all relevant issues will hurt you.
- Be prepared.
- Ask questions if you don't understand something. Prepare a list of questions before you see the banker.
- Have a definite plan but be flexible.
- Keep your banker informed of any changes in the business.
- Negotiate rates after you've presented the loan request. Be sure to research the market rates.

Don'ts:

- Be impatient.
- Make promises you can't keep.
- Ask "how much" you can borrow.
- Negotiate interest rates over the telephone.
- Spend the money before you ask for it.
- Change banks solely for a better interest rate, unless your bank is not competitive.
- Ever surprise your banker.

Preparing For Your Visit with a Lender

Documentation requirements may vary. Check with the lender for a list of requirements you must supply.

Common requirements include the following:

- Letter of Request which includes:
  1. Purpose of the loan.
  2. History of the business.
  3. Amount of loan.
  4. How the loan will be repaid.
  5. Amount of investment in the business by the owner (s).

- Financial statements for three years (existing businesses).
- Schedule of term debts (existing businesses).
- Aging of accounts receivable and payable (existing businesses).
- Projected opening-day balance sheet (new businesses).
- Lease details.
- Projections of income, expenses and cash flow as well as the assumptions.
- Personal financial statements on the principal owners.
- Resume of each principal owner and manager.
- Business Plan (new businesses).

Pitfalls and Success Tips

Pitfalls:

1. Submitting an incomplete package. Lenders will quickly decline the request.

2. Relying on one lender to make a deal. Always keep your options open. Shop your deal through multiple lenders. Each lender differs in values. One may value their customer and keep an open line of communication, whereas another lender may not see the value in communicating with their customer or getting the deal processed as soon as possible.

3. Asking for too much money. Know how much money is required for your business need. If you ask for too much, you will likely be denied. If you ask for too little, the lender begins to ask more questions and won't see the potential in the business or its ability to sustain.

4. Asking for money with a "D" credit, bad business plan and not enough down payment. The biggest mistake a business owner can make when trying to secure capital with a lender, is to apply for a loan with a less than perfect credit score under 700, numerous late payments, recent collections, and less than 20 percent cash down payment.

5. Harassing a lender. Try to avoid making more than one call a week to follow up on a pending request. Lenders don't take too kindly to prospects calling them daily interrupting their work time.

Success Secrets

1. Build relationships with more than one lender. The more relationships you have with lenders the greater your chances are of getting a loan and learning the inside trades of what it takes to secure a loan.

2. Have a concise business plan. Make sure the business plan is to the point, contains detailed information in each section, is not more than 25 pages in length, and is consistent with your mission.

3. Know your funding options. If you have gotten this far, that means you are well informed on what types of loans are available to you, how they work, and which is more suitable for your business needs.

4. Attend network meetings where investors and bankers meet. The best way to build relationships with lenders is to get personal. Look up banker's associations for a list of networking groups in your area and also visit www.lava.org for investor meetings and events.

5. Prepare financial assumptions. Lenders want to know where and how the money will be spent. One of the biggest mistakes borrowers make is not including "financial assumptions." This section is most important and one that is viewed immediately when the loan is requested. You should outline dollar for dollar what assumptions you made in each area of your financial forecasts.

Words of Wisdom from Lenders that Service You:

Maintain conservative business practice, keep expenses low and reduce expenses accordingly. Have a clear and concise business plan, which can help the business pull through and sustain during a slow period. Lastly, communicate with your banker.

- ***Cal Naulls, First Vice President- Regional Manager, Community Bank of Santa Clarita Valley***

Prepare a comprehensive business plan including five-year projections. Take advantage of SBA financing programs and their resources. "We all have dreams but we must prepare a road map which coincides with the business vision."

-Willie Pleitez, Branch Manager, Mission Valley Bank of Santa Clarita

CHAPTER 7

REFINING THE BUSINESS PLAN

Refining The Business Plan To Meet Specific Needs

In addition to the standard business plan, you may need to refine the plan to include specific information and details.

For Raising Capital

For Bankers

Bankers want assurance of orderly repayment. If you intend using this plan to present to lenders, include:

- Amount of loan
- How the funds will be used
- What this will accomplish—how will it make the business stronger?
- Requested repayment terms (number of years to repay). You will probably not have much negotiating room on interest rate but may be able to negotiate a longer repayment term, which will help cash flow.
- Collateral offered, and a list of all existing liens against collateral

Investors have a different perspective. They are looking for dramatic growth, and they expect to share in the rewards:

- Funds needed in two to five years
- How the company will use the funds, and what this will accomplish for growth.
- Estimated return on investment
- Exit strategy for investors (buyback, sale, or IPO)
- Percent of ownership that you will give up to investors
- Milestones or conditions that you will accept
- Financial reporting to be provided
- Involvement of investors on the board or in management

For Type of Business

Manufacturing

- Planned production levels
- Anticipated levels of direct production costs and indirect (overhead) costs—how do these compare to industry averages (if available)?
- Prices per product line
- Gross profit margin, overall and for each product line
- Production/capacity limits of planned physical plant
- Production/capacity limits of equipment
- Purchasing and inventory management procedures
- New products under development or anticipated to come online after startup

Service Businesses

Service businesses sell intangible products. They are usually more flexible than other types of businesses, but they also have higher labor costs and generally very little in fixed assets:

- What are the key competitive factors in this industry?
- Your prices
- Methods used to set prices
- System of production management
- Quality control procedures. Standard or accepted industry quality standards.
- How will you measure labor productivity?
- Percent of work subcontracted to other firms. Will you make a profit on subcontracting?
- Credit, payment, and collections policies and procedures
- Strategy for keeping client base

High Technology Companies

Economic outlook for the industry:

- Will the company have information systems in place to manage rapidly changing prices, costs, and markets?
- Will you be on the cutting edge with your products and services?

- What is the status of research and development? And what is required to:
  - ❖ Bring product/service to market?
  - ❖ Keep the company competitive?

How does the company:

- Protect intellectual property?
- Avoid technological obsolescence?
- Supply necessary capital?
- Retain key personnel?

High-tech companies sometimes have to operate for a long time without profits and sometimes even without sales. If this fits your situation, a banker probably will not want to lend to you. Venture capitalists may invest, but your story must be very good. You must do longer-term financial forecasts to show when profit take-off is expected to occur. And your assumptions must be well documented and well argued.

Retail Business

- Company image
- Pricing:
  - ❖ Explain markup policies.
  - ❖ Prices should be profitable, competitive, and in accordance with company image.
- Inventory:
  - ❖ Selection and price should be consistent with company image.
  - ❖ Inventory level: Find industry average numbers for annual inventory turnover rate (available in RMA book). Multiply your initial inventory investment by the average turnover rate. The result should be at least equal to your projected first year's cost of goods sold. If it is not, you may not have enough budgeted for startup inventory.
- Customer service policies: These should be competitive and in accord with company image.
- Location: Does it give the exposure that you need? Is it convenient for customers? Is it consistent with company image?
- Promotion: Methods used and costs. Does it project a consistent company image?
- Credit: Do you extend credit to customers? If yes, do you really need to, and do you factor the cost into prices?

Why Banks
Say No

And How To Get <u>Your</u> Loan Application Approved!

Is Your Business Under-financed?

Join the club.

As we move from an industrial to an information and service society, a new generation of companies is spawning. Entrepreneurs no longer have to buy expensive equipment or inventories to get their businesses started. They rely instead on their intellectual capital. Two simple examples are software developers and consultants.

These entrepreneurs depend more on their own skills, time, and knowledge than any other "fixed" asset.

The good news is that these types of businesses are easy to set up and have minimal associated costs. The bad news is that because you don't have many fixed assets, traditional lending institutions like banks don't know how to valuate your business.

You can have rapidly growing revenues and still be under-financed. In fact, the statistics show that if you are a high growth company, you are more likely to be under-financed!

Overall, 20.7% of companies are under-financed. But when you look at companies that have grown their revenues by 20% or more over the past three years, you'll find that 30.8% of them are under -financed!

It is obvious from this data that it is the young, high performing companies that are currently experiencing the greatest difficulty in obtaining the financing they need to operate their businesses.

Many entrepreneurs are so discouraged that they don't even apply for financing. In 2000, only 60% of small and medium sized companies tried to raise capital. Only 53.8% of businesses with zero to four employees applied for financing. As a result, in the late 1980's, only 15% of entrepreneurs were concerned over their financial situation. Fast forward to 2002 and that number rises to almost 40%! So why are these numbers so discouraging? Most entrepreneurs only turn to one source of potential capital: Banks.

Banks Don't Like Small Loans

Banks typically have a $200,000 threshold loan limit.
Over the past 15 years, the number of loans given to companies over this $200,000 limit has grown over 30%. On the other hand, loans given to entrepreneurs who need less than $200,000 has been stagnant for the past 15 years. If you look at this number in real terms and account for inflation, the loans given to small businesses has actually been decreasing.

As Chuck Loewen from Online Business Systems says, "Understand the real role of a financial institution is to lease safe capital to low-risk borrowers. Entrepreneurs, full of vim and vigor mistake the bank's role as the entity that will share the risks with them to see the entrepreneur's dream come true. Not so. Always understand you are the entrepreneur, he or she is the banker."

Key Loan Factors

According to the Canadian Federation of Independent Business (CFIB), there are four key factors that can dramatically increase your chance of obtaining a bank loan. They are: account manager turnover, business experience, business banking services, and size of company.

Account Manager Turnover
Your bank account manager is responsible for understanding your business and going to bat for you within the organization when you need a loan approved. If she does not have an established long term relationship with you it will be difficult to get her to pull strings for you.

The chance of you being rejected for a bank loan depending on how many account managers you have is as follows: What do you mean by account managers?

- One account manager: 7.1% rejection rate

- Two account managers: 8.5% rejection rate

- Three account managers: 16.3% rejection rate
- Four or more account managers: 22.8% rejection rate.

Develop a good relationship with your banker early. Talk to her before you need the money and she'll be there for you when you actually go for the loan.

Business Experience
Banks want to lend money to established businesses with a track record of experience. The reason is pretty simple: you have proven that you can achieve certain results which make your future projections less risky. If you can show that you have done it before it is easier to have faith that you can do it again compared to a startup with no experience.

Banks prefer companies that have been around for 10 years or more. These companies:

- Get rejected for loans over 50% less frequently than in-experienced firms

- Pay around 0.4% less interest on their loans

If you do not have 10 years of company history, as most entrepreneurs do not, point to your other experiences that will help give you credibility. Maybe you worked as an employee in a small company and helped double their sales. Perhaps you ran another small business and made it profitable within 6 months. When you do not have the company track record, the banker immediately flags your business as having an increased risk of not being able to pay back the loan. You need to show whatever experience you can from related jobs or companies to reduce the banker's perceived risk and maximize the chance of you securing the loan.

Business Banking Services
Let's say you run a website design company. You have two clients. One client uses your services on a regular basis. Every month she comes to you with a plan to update her site and she sees you as a trusted business partner. The other client had you set up her site but you have not heard from her for six months for any improvements or updates. She sees you as a necessary evil to getting her business going and wants to deal with you only when she absolutely has to. Now, say both clients come to you and want site changes but neither can pay up front. They want you to credit their account and they offer to pay you in a couple of months. Assuming you could only grant the credit to one person, who would it be?
The answer is obviously the first client who uses you on a regular basis and sees you as a trusted business partner.

Banks work the same way. The more you use their business services and the more you are in contact with them, the more they get to know you, the more they want to keep you as a client, and the more likely they will give accept your loan application over other businesses, with all else being equal.

Develop this relationship by setting up all of your accounts with one bank. Use them for your checking account, your savings account, your credit cards, your loans and lines of credit, and every other business banking service you end up using. When you sit down with your account manager for your loan application and she pulls up your account history on her computer, you want her to think "Wow. This client is really using a lot of our services. I want to do as much as I can to make sure I can keep her at our bank."

Size Of Company
Finally, the size of your company will be a crucial factor in the bank's decision to give you a loan or not. Again, remember that banks like lending safe capital to low-risk borrowers. They do not like high-risk entrepreneurs. Therefore, the bigger you are, the safer you are and the more likely you are to get your loan. The loan rejection numbers by size of your company look like this:

- 0 to 4 employees: 13.6% rejection rate
- 5 to 19 employees: 10.7% rejection rate
- 20 to 49 employees: 6.0% rejection rate
- 50 to 99 employees: 4.1% rejection rate
- Over 100 employees: 2.5% rejection rate

Who Makes The Decisions?

When applying for a loan it is also important to know who is going to be making the final decision as to whether you get accepted or rejected.

According to recent CFIB data, the decision maker breakdown looks like this:

- 36% of decisions are made by the head or regional offices
- 31% of decisions are unknown who the final decision maker is
- 25% of decisions are made by the local branch office
- 8% of decisions are made by automated credit scoring models

What is interesting to note is that most of the decisions are still made by real people, not computers. And people make emotional decisions, not always rational ones. By presenting your case and letting the decision maker get to know you and your story, you can increase the chance that they will say yes.

Why Banks Say No

Finally, according to a CFIB survey of entrepreneurs who have applied for bank loans, here are the most common reasons the banks give them for why their application was rejected:

- 26.6%: Too much outstanding debt
- 26.6%: Lack of owner equity
- 24.8%: Insufficient cash flow
- 17.2%: Too new in business
- 13.7%: Poor industry conditions
- 11.6%: No reasons were given
- 7.8%: Products not considered profitable
- 4.1%: Inadequate business plan
- 4.0%: Environmental risk factors

These are the major warning signs that bankers will look out for before approving your loan. Before submitting your application you must try as hard as you can do anticipate and counter possible arguments in each of these areas.

One disturbing fact is that over 11% of entrepreneurs who get their loan applications rejected are not given a reason from the banks as to why this happened. The most important thing you can do if you get rejected is to listen to your banker. Always find out the reasons why you got turned down. Then ask what you can do over the next couple of weeks or months to improve your business so that they will accept your application.

Working with banks is not always an easy thing for entrepreneurs to do. They are, however, going to be important to the growth and success of your business. Take the approach that you would rather be their friends than their adversaries and work with them to get them to trust you and want your business.

Good luck and keep building the company of your dreams!
Evan.

Evan Carmichael helps entrepreneurs who are tired of struggling and not having money to grow their businesses. He can be contacted at evan@evancarmichael.com. You can visit his website at: www.evancarmichael.com for additional articles and information.

APPENDIX

APPENDIX 1

Sample
Executive Summary

TRAILWAY DESIGNS is a high-end design and remodeling company with a reputation for integrity, quality craftsmanship, and excellence in management. In three years, annual sales have increased be well over two million dollars.

TRAILWAY DESIGNS was formed by Kandy Moore as a Sole Proprietorship in March 2000. In 2001 a combination of activities involving residential design, consulting, and general construction brought Gross Sales of $300,000.

The company has experienced steady growth since its inception, and incorporated in December 2002. In 2002 Gross Sales of $750,000 were achieved. In 2004, signed contracts show that Gross Sales are expected to be $2,100,000 (see Appendix 2, current Backlog).

The company located in leased premises at 27556 Sarrahfields, Woodchuck, WY 29986. Its activities fall under the Standard Industrial Classification SIC 1521 and 1522. The owners are Kandy Moore and Irina Geosoff.

TRAILWAY DESIGNS is involved in four distinct activities:

1. Architectural Design
2. Residential & Light Commercial Construction
3. Property Services
4. Retail Floor Coverings (see Appendix 4).

Eighty to ninety percent of the Gross Sales are in design and construction. At the moment (May 2004), there are 35 permanent employees on the payroll and 15 subcontracted workers excluding subcontracting companies (see Appendix 5 for resumes).

The company's Short Term Objectives (within the next three years) are to increase activity in all divisions, and to achieve an annual profit, net after taxes, of $250,000 by 2005. Its long-term objectives are: to maintain the level of current business achieved up to 2005 then move into historical restorations, more light commercial work, and increased new custom home construction.

To implement these objectives the company needs:

1. A loan of $100,000 at Prime plus 2%. This loan to be used for current near term expenses including payroll, advertising and leaseholds. It will be repaid in five years.
2. A line of credit of $50,000 to take advantage of discounts available, avoid associated penalties, and expand into high profit areas requiring positive cash flow.

The prospects for TRAILWAY DESIGNS' continued growth are excellent, with 2000 construction and design contracts underway already exceeding $550,000 (see Appendix 2, Backlog 2000).

For equity the company has assets of $227,000 (see Appendix 9, Balance Sheet as of 04/17/2003). Additionally, the company's owners are willing to offer as collateral a second mortgage on a residence with an estimated equity of $150,000. The address of this residence is 2798 Sand Canyon, Mt. Vernon, CA 91304.

The company's overall objective is to satisfy that market segment that demands integrity and quality construction, and to maintain a steady growth in sales volume that will sustain the company for twenty years. Kandy Moore has enhanced her reputation to the point where many architects regard the company as the recommended choice with their clients due to the excellence of its craftsmen and management.

Market research shows that the population in Springfield has increased by 200,000 between 1985 and 2003. This increase in population brought about an increase of 19,850 new single-family homes valued at over three billion dollars. This increase gives the area over 128,000 existing homes as a potential remodeling market. Demographic estimates published by the State Office of Financial Management, 2002, indicate that an additional 20,000 persons will need to be housed between 2002 and 2020.

TRAILWAY DESIGNS intends to pursue this market vigorously. (See Appendix 7 for data on anticipated changes in the population of the county).

Financial Objectives
The financial objectives of TRAILWAY DESIGNS over the next few years are as follows:

	2005	**2005-2010**
Sales	$7,000,000	$10,000,000
Net Income after Tax	$500,000	$1,000,000

Please review the enclosed business plan and loan proposal, and of course feel free to ask for any additional information or explanations you may want. I will call you in about one week's time to arrange an appointment so that we can discuss the loan in person.

I look forward to a mutually profitable relationship with the Tallbost Bank.

APPENDIX 2

WADE
INSTITUTE

Loan Packaging Check List

____ **Personal Federal Tax Returns**, including all schedules (C, etc.), for the past three years

____ **Personal financial Statement**

____ **Management Resume** (for all directors, officers, and key employees)

____ **Complete Business Federal Tax Returns**, including all schedules, for the past three years.

____ **Business Financial Statement** (including balance sheets & income statement, for the past 3 year ends

____ **Interim Financial Statement**, including balance sheet and income statement, dated with in the past 60 days

____ **Business Debt Schedule** (dated same as the interim financial statement, with total matching that on the interim financial statement

____ **Accounts Receivable Aging**, dated same as the interim financial statement, with totals matching those on the interim financial statement

____ **Accounts Payable Aging,** dated same as the interim financial statement, with totals matching those on the interim financial statement

____ **Profit and Loss Projections** for a one year period

____ **Business Trade References**

____ **Credit Reports** (business and personal)

____ **Adequate Notice Form**

____ **Business Plan**

____ **Loan Application**

____ **Loan Request Form**

____ **History of Business**

For Real Estate Refinance:

____ Copy of Note (s) to be refinanced

____ Copy of Deed (s) of Trust to be refinanced

____ Copy of most recent payment stub (s)/statement (s) with evidence of current balance of the note (s) to be refinanced

Real Estate Purchase:

____ Copy of Purchase Agreement

Business Purchase:

____ **Complete Business Federal Tax Returns**, including all schedules, for the past three years (signed & dated by the seller)

____ **Business Financial Statements** including balance sheets and income statements for the past three year ends (signed and dated by the seller)

____ **Interim Financial Statements**, including balance sheet and income statement, dated within the past 60 days (signed & dated by seller)

____ **Copy of Buy/Sell Agreement** (Purchase Agreement)
(If business is a Franchise, a copy of the Franchise Agreement and a copy of the FTC Disclosure Report on Franchisors will be required)

Construction:

____ Application for Approval of Contractor

____ Information on Work in Progress

____ Construction Cost Breakdown

Equipment/Inventory Purchase:

____ Detailed list of machinery/equipment & inventory to be purchased. List should indicate the estimated costs and set-up expenses

Glossary

Assets: Tangible items with an attached value to offset debt. They are generally divided into two groups — current assets and fixed (long-term) assets. They are usually presented in order of liquidity, with current assets (cash and those that will be converted to cash within one year) appearing first

Business Ratios: Identify key relationships between financial data and allow you to monitor liquidity, profitability, and efficiency.

Capital Infusion: Type of capital secured from a lender or investor.

Collateralized: Securing a loan with equipment or other forms of assets, which can be liquidated to pay a debt.

Conversion Cycles: Capable of converting assets (cash, accounts receivable, inventory) during any given period.

Cost of Goods (COGs): Materials used to manufacture or produce goods.

Current Ratio: The current ratio is a way of looking at your working capital and measuring your short-term solvency. The ratio is in the format x:y, where x is the amount of all current assets and y is the amount of all current liabilities.

Debt Financing: Means borrowing money that is to be repaid over a period of time, usually with interest. Debt financing can be either short-term (full repayment due in less than one year) or long-term (repayment due over more than one year).

Equity: Stockholders' equity (or owner's equity or net worth)

Equity Financing: Is an exchange of money for a share of business ownership. This form of financing allows you to obtain funds without incurring debt. The major disadvantage to equity financing is the dilution of your ownership interest and the possible loss of control as a result of sharing ownership with additional investors.

Factoring: The conversion of a company's business accounts receivable (invoices) into immediate cash by selling those invoices at a discount.

Fixed Assets: Expense amounts that don't change.

Injection: Down payment toward a loan.

Liabilities: Debt. Liabilities are normally presented in order of their claim on the company's assets.

Uniform Commercial Code (UCC): Serves to perfect a security interest in named collateral and establish priority in case of debtor default or bankruptcy.

Variable Assets: Expenses that fluctuate in costs.

Working Capital: The amount of current assets that are not financed by current liabilities. Also used to maintain a proper ratio of current assets to current liabilities; otherwise the liquidity of the company may be compromised.

Subordinate Debt: Subordinated debt has a lower priority than other bonds of the issuer in case of liquidation during bankruptcy, below the liquidator, government tax authorities and senior debt holders in the hierarchy of creditors. Because subordinated debt is repayable after other debts have been paid, they are more risky for the lender of the money. It is unsecured and has lesser priority than that of an additional debt claim on the same asset.

Referrals & Resources

Connie Sparks
President
Wade Institute, LLC
27305 W. Live Oak Rd., A-421
Castaic, CA 91384
Office: 661 208-8229
www.wadeinstitute.org

LaKisha Gant
Loan Officer
CDC Small Business Finance
1650 Iowa Avenue, Suite 150
Riverside, CA 92507
Direct Number: 951-905-5702
Cell Number: 951 543-1138
lakisha.gant@yahoo.com

Cal Naulls
First Vice President- Regional Manager
Community Bank of Santa Clarita
28494 Westinghouse Pl., Ste.308
Santa Clarita, CA 91355
Office: 661 295-2850
Fax: 661 295-2841
www.cbank.com

Meritus Ventures, LP
Licensed RBIC Website: http://www.meritusventures.com
Phone: 606-864-5175
Fax: 606-864-5194)

Lenders
www.sba.gov /Existing Businesses
www.jfla.org / Start-ups
www.accion.com / Start-ups
www.telacu.com

Alternative Financing
www.1stcommercialcredit.com / AR Financing
www.business.com / AR Financing
www.funding.merchantequip.com / Credit Card Financing

Investor Networks

www.gobignetwork.com
www.fundingpost.com
www.bedzzinninc.com
www.breadstreet.com
www.advisorgarage.com
www.lava.org

Certifications and Government Contracting

Federal
Caltrans and Department of Defense (DOD)
www.fedbizoppps.gov

State
Certifications: 8a, Small Disadvantage Business Enterprise
Disadvantaged Business Enterprise (DBE), Disabled Veteran business Enterprise (DVBE), Small Business Certification
www.sba.gov
www.pd.dgs.ca.gov

LA County
Certification: County Vendor, Minority Business Enterprise (MBE)Women Owned Business Enterprise (WBE)
www.lacounty.gov
http://camisvr.co.la.ca.us/webven
(877) 669-CBES

Apply for DUNS Number
www.dnb.com

Apply for Centralized Contractor Registration (CCR) www.ccr.gov

Obtain NAICS Code
North American Industry Classification System (NAICS)
http://www.sba.gov/sizeNAICS-cover-page.htm

About the Author

Connie Sparks Author, Business Strategist, and Trainer is president of the Wade Institute, LLC, a Business Development and Training Company. Wade Institute (WIN) provides an array of business planning products and services, which include process improvement management, and operational audits. She is recognized as an advocate for educating and training women, promoting success, growth, and leadership. Moreover, through community partnerships she has trained more than 4,000 business owners and executives collectively throughout California.

Ms. Sparks serves as a Board of Director for the Santa Clarita Domestic Violence Center where she takes pride in creating opportunities and supporting disadvantage women and children. She is committed to building communities and the workforce. Additionally she works closely with the Santa Clarita Valley Small Business Development Center as a Business Advisor and Trainer and an Intermediary Technical Assistant with the Small Business Administration (SBA) and Superior Financial Group.

Her background includes more than fifteen years in the business service industry, nine years in management, program development and human resources, collectively. Her education includes a degree in Business Management and Human Resource, and she holds a credential in Business Communication and Computer Applications.

Ms. Sparks's published work include ***The Survival Skills for African American Women, Where's The Money: Big Dollars to Do Big Business Like the Big Boys*** and the ***Entrepreneur's Guide for Starting a Business***. She's been featured in various news articles circulated internationally, discussing her views on domestic violence, entrepreneurship and business development.

She has been honored by Toastmasters International (President's Distinguished Award 2002), The For You Network- National Association of Female Executives (NAFE) (Business Woman of the Year 2006), (Best Corporate Environment Award 2006), and (Sphere of Influence Award 2007), the Los Angeles Business Journal (Women Who Make A Difference 2007, 2009), and the U.S. Small Business Administration (Home-Based Business Champion Award 2009).

Notes: